WHAT

AN ALL NATIONS BOOKLET

What in the World is God Doing?

MARTIN GOLDSMITH

MARC
Eastbourne

First published 1991

Front cover photo: Tony Stone Photolibrary – London

British Library Cataloguing in Publication Data

Goldsmith, Martin *1934–*
    What in the world is God doing?
    1. Christianity
    I. Title
    200

    ISBN 1–85424–138–9

Printed in Great Britain for
MARC, an imprint of Monarch Publications Ltd
1 St Anne's Road, Eastbourne, E Sussex BN21 3UN by
Richard Clay Ltd, Bungay, Suffolk
Typeset by J&L Composition Ltd, Filey, North Yorkshire

THE ALL NATIONS SERIES

All Nations Booklets aim to:
1. Provide basic teaching on various aspects of mission
2. Raise awareness of the importance of mission in Western churches
3. Stimulate support for mission through prayer and action
4. Help churches in the multi-cultural West to learn from the experiences of churches worldwide?

CONTENTS

1
IT'S GOD'S WORLD AND GOD WORKS IN IT

The global village

Times have changed remarkably in the thirty years since my wife and I enjoyed three weeks on a liner en route to Singapore as new missionaries. Asia seemed then a very long way away, and most people knew little about such distant parts of the world.

In 1960 television was still an unusual addition to the home, so few people had seen live pictures of remote countries. Air travel was expensive and long sea journeys were required if you needed to visit other continents.

Today things are very different. Relatively cheap air travel has opened the door for multitudes to visit other countries. Not only do missionaries, business people and diplomats enjoy this opportunity, but the travel agents beckon the tourist to adventurous holidays in all parts of the world. Many Europeans have had holidays in the Muslim countries of North Africa or Turkey. A few have ventured into very different cultural situations in

Nepal, India or even remote tribal areas. The exotic beauties of Thailand, Malaysia, Indonesia or Japan are no longer tied to the missionaries' slide shows, but have become the living experience of many. Television has brought the whole world into our sitting rooms.

No longer can we afford to remain in blinkered insularity. What happens in one part of the world affects us all. Political change in Eastern Europe influences our political and economic climate. Marxist communism has been fearfully discredited —how will that affect the thinking of our university and college lecturers? Will it change the whole philosophical and religious approach in Western Europe? New tensions in the Middle East and the Gulf affect racial relations in Britain as Muslims voice their disillusionment with our government's policies and feel that the crusading spirit of imperialism threatens the Muslim world again. Our stock market and economy shiver at every uncertainty on the world scene. No country or people today can live in isolation like ostriches with their heads in the sand—we all depend on each other.

So the Christian needs to understand what is happening in the world.

God's world

The Bible never lets us forget that God created the world, everything in it and all people of every race and background. Again and again the Bible reminds us that God is not some irrelevant old gentleman sitting impotently in heaven while things on earth develop independently of him.

From the Bible it is clear that he is the sovereign Lord who controls the movements of history with his own purposes in mind. He not only controls those who believe in him and desire to follow his will, but also has the power to use men like Pharaoh, Nebuchadnezzar and Cyrus as his instruments. The rise and fall of empires is in his hands.

What are his purposes in history? What should we be looking for, and thinking of, as we read our newspapers, watch our television and pray about the world?

In Colossians 1:16 we read that everything was created by the Lord and for him. The fundamental purpose of this world is to give him pleasure. As Christians we long that all nations would so honour Jesus Christ that they would live for his glory and pleasure. At present we all seem to live for the satisfaction of our own selfish desires and to bolster our pride—this is true of nation states as well as individual human beings. What a difference it would make if everybody and every society or nation made it their aim to please the Lord.

What does it mean in practice to live for God's pleasure?

The Bible talks much about God's kingdom as his purpose and our goal. In Romans 14:17 Paul lists three fundamental characteristics of God's kingdom. Righteousness, peace and joy in the Holy Spirit are what God looks for in this world and what we should work and pray for. Paul goes on to declare that these characteristics are the true marks of serving Christ. Without Jesus Christ it will prove impossible to develop lives and societies where purity, holiness and godly righteousness reign. Peace too will elude us. Broken or strained relationships, racial tensions, class divisions, generation gaps, international selfishness and even warfare—all these tragic realities will be only too common if Jesus Christ is not acknowledged as King. Without the Holy Spirit there can be no deep, constant joy in life.

Evangelism is therefore essential to help people to honour and please the Lord. But God does not only look for people to come to faith in Christ for their own salvation. We are also called to serve the Lord in personal and social righteousness, in peace and peaceful relationships, with an infectious joy in the Holy Spirit.

In this book we want to look at what God is doing in the various parts of the world today. We shall want to see whether people are coming to faith in Christ and thus beginning to live for his pleasure and glory. We shall therefore want to see whether his church is growing numerically. But we shall also want to see whether these three marks of the presence of God's kingdom are in evidence.

Worldwide vision

There is always a danger that Christians become so preoccupied with their own country and people that they fail to gain an active interest in the rest of the world, or even in other races within their own country.

Such a narrow vision loses sight of God's deep concern for the whole world. God's great desire is that all peoples should come to faith in Jesus Christ and so enjoy the resurrection life in oneness with God the Father.

Narrow insularity is no new problem. The New

Testament church faced the pressing question of whether Gentiles should be evangelised and accepted into the church. The early Jewish Christians knew that God had created the whole world, not just Israel, but still they thought of him as primarily the God of Israel. They knew in theory that the kingdom of the Messiah was to be for all peoples, but they looked for a Messiah who would save his own people Israel. Much of the New Testament is written therefore to show that the good news of Jesus Christ is indeed for all peoples, and that Christians should share the gospel with all—Jews and Gentiles of all races everywhere.

As the apostle to the Gentiles, Paul is particularly keen to show that his calling is a right one. For example, in Romans he argues that people of all races, Jews and Gentiles alike, are under the power of sin (Rom 1:1–3:20). He then shows that God has provided a universally available solution to this universal problem of sin. The answer is in the death of Jesus for our sins, the benefit of which we receive through faith in Christ rather than through following the commands of the Jewish law (eg Rom 3:28). Faith in Christ can be exercised by all peoples, not just by Jews. If the Jewish law had been the means of salvation, then the church would have remained exclusively for Jews and those Gentiles who joined themselves to the people of Israel as proselytes. But God has provided the way of redemption for all peoples in Jesus Christ and it is our task to share that good news throughout the world.

As Paul's companion in part of his missionary journeys, Luke shares that same international vision. We see this particularly clearly in his Acts of the Apostles. Luke's thesis is that the Holy Spirit's power sends Christ's disciples out as witnesses not only among Jews in Jerusalem and Judea, but also among the half-Jewish half-Gentile Samaritans and then among Gentiles 'to the end of the earth' (Acts 1:8). This is clear from the structure of the book.

The first seven chapters show the church's witness among Jews only. Then in Acts 8 we are given two bridges to span the fearful gulf between the Jews and the Gentiles. Philip evangelises the Samaritans and is also led by the Spirit to bring the Ethiopian eunuch to faith in Jesus as Messiah. The eunuch was almost certainly an African Gentile, but we know he was already closely related to Israel in that he was going to worship in the Jerusalem Temple and was reading the Hebrew Scriptures. Only after these two half-way houses between Jews and Gentiles does Luke tell the story of the conversion of Paul, the apostle to the Gentiles. In Acts 10 and 11 we read of the Gentile Cornelius coming to faith in Jesus Christ and then in Acts 13 Paul and Barnabas make the crucial declaration 'we turn to the Gentiles' (13:46). From then on the expansion of the church among the Gentiles begins to unfold—and it has continued to widen and grow throughout these past two thousand years. We today inherit that history and take our place in God's purposes for the preaching of the gospel to all peoples everywhere.

Dark clouds and silver linings

When we examine the development of the church worldwide through the centuries and look at what God is doing in our generation, it is easy to be unbalanced. Some of us are natural optimists and enthusiasts, so are tempted to take note of the growth of the church and revival movements. But we may fail to take seriously the areas of defeat or stagnation. Others of us tend towards pessimism, so may concentrate on the fearful failures of the church and the overwhelming needs everywhere. Some of us believe that every small grey cloud is surrounded by wonderful silver linings, while others note that depressingly heavy grey clouds overshadow the sadly small silver linings.

We see this tension in the biblical teaching of the kingdom of God. Jesus announced that the kingdom had come and was now present among us. In the person of Jesus Christ the kingdom is already here. And yet he also taught his disciples to pray 'thy kingdom come' because the fullness of the kingdom is still a future hope which we pray and work for. The kingdom starts very small, grows and finally will be brought to its complete glory. Even Jesus himself, the King of the kingdom, came as a tiny baby, grew 'in wisdom and in stature, and in favour with God and man' (Lk 2:52) and only then ascended to the fullness of his glory in the presence of his Father. The New Testament church also started very small. It began with a tiny handful of insignificant, unknown men and a few women. But it grew. The Book of Acts records how more and more believers were added to the church. And it spread from its purely Jewish base to reach out to the neighbouring Gentile peoples of South Europe, North Africa and the Middle East. Then it gradually widened its outreach to India, China and North Europe. Today the church is to be found in every continent, although not yet in every race or every geographical area. The church still needs to expand.

Each individual Christian also starts the Christian life in weakness—the New Testament picture is of our being born again. We are always born small! Next the Christian should grow in grace, holiness and knowledge of the Lord. Finally we shall be perfectly holy as the Lord himself is holy; we shall love him fully; we shall know him perfectly.

God has already done great things, but there remains much which he has not yet done in each of us personally, in the church and in the world which he created and longs to bring to perfect redemption.

This combination of 'already' and 'not yet' in the work and life of God's kingdom leaves us with a certain tension. It is good to rejoice in all that God has already done for us, for our church, for the church worldwide and for the world. But if we forget our failure to achieve the fullness of God's glory, then we can easily become proudly triumphalistic and smug. We need to be deeply aware of our need for God to work more fully. But if we forget to be thankful for what God has already done, then we can become depressed and ungrateful.

When you read the mission reports of some Christians today, you get a glorious sense of revival breaking out everywhere and the church triumphant by the Holy Spirit. While it is true that our God is wonderfully at work, there also remain areas of the world where it is difficult to rejoice so confidently and in every part of the world there remains a considerable 'not yet' in the working of God's kingdom.

On the other hand there are other Christians whose mission reports underline the overwhelming need of unevangelised multitudes and the shocking weaknesses of the church spiritually, morally and socially. This apparent realism sometimes fails to give God the glory for the great things he has already done in and through his people. Realism should not only be negative.

In this book I will try to be truthful and not propagandist. I believe that our Lord Jesus is the truth (Jn 14:6) and therefore it is vitally important for the Christian to be like our Lord and Master. Like him we should be careful that our words are totally true. Biased or one-sided reporting will not convey 'the truth, the whole truth and nothing but the truth'. We believe that our God is perfect in what he does and in his timing. There is no need either to embroider our reports of what he has already wonderfully done, or emphasise unduly what he has not yet done. We can trust him to do it in his own perfect time and way.

Throughout this book many statistics will be quoted, but it should be noted that all mission statistics remain highly unreliable. For this reason I shall not follow the pattern of many who write and speak about mission and the church in the various parts of the world. Although neat diagrams communicate clearly and graphically how many Christians there are in relation to the followers of other religions, they also oversimplify and force us to produce statistics which cannot actually be discovered. Graphs of the growth of particular churches can misrepresent the realities of the working of God's Spirit in promoting his kingdom. While I remain grateful for the statistics, graphs and diagrams in other people's writings, the multitude of question marks I have added in the margins of such books and articles has compelled me to refuse to yield to pressures to add such aids to this book. Genuine truth must remain more important than particular styles of communication.

2

TO THE JEW FIRST

What is God doing among Jews?

Since Jesus and all the original Christians were Jews, the church is rooted in Jewish soil. With his repeated phrase 'to the Jew first' (Rom 1:16, 2:9–10), Paul, the apostle to the Gentiles, underlines how vitally significant the Jews are in God's eyes. So it seems right to start our world tour with a brief chapter on what God is doing among Jews.

Behind everything that relates to Jews hangs the spectre of the Holocaust. The nightmare of the Nazi concentration camps and gas chambers haunts us. In just a few years six million Jews, one third of the total race, died in an appalling way. Almost every European Jew today lost relatives in Hitler's climactic horror.

Some Gentile Christians ask therefore whether it can be right for them to evangelise among Jews. With the background of the Holocaust, has the church any right to preach to Jews? Christian Zionists have chosen to show friendship to the state and people of Israel, but deny the need for evangelism. They are not unique in this stance. Some other Christians note how Israel has failed to show proper justice in its dealings with the Palestinians, so they side with the Arabs against the Jews: for them Jewish evangelism is secondary to questions of political justice. Many more liberal Christians in recent years have also opposed evangelism of Jews, claiming that Jews have their own covenant and way to God. They cannot see why Jews need Jesus.

But to be faithful to their Lord, Christians must evangelise all peoples because they all, including the Jews, need the good news of Jesus, the Messiah.

Christians must evangelise

Compromise of biblical truth is never right, even if the motive is one of apparent humility and love. As Christians we need to recognise the evils which have in the past been perpetrated in the name of Christ and repent of all such anti-semitism. Nevertheless with sensitive humility we are called to share the good news which we have received and which has changed our lives. We believe that in the life, death and resurrection of Jesus Christ, God has given us not only eternal life and hope, but also a present enjoyment of his forgiving love and his life-giving Spirit. To keep such good news to ourselves and deny it to our Jewish friends would in fact be a new form of anti-semitism. As a Jewish Christian myself I felt deeply sad when a Swedish missionary to Israel attacked all evangelism among Jews and told me that I ought not to be a Christian. What would Peter, Paul, James, John and other

early Jewish Christians have thought if they had
known that later Gentile Christians would have
denied them the right to have the gospel of Jesus
presented to them?

Happily the God of Israel is still at work and
giving both Jewish and Gentile Christians a
renewed vision for evangelism among Jews.

Jews need Jesus

We have already noted in the previous chapter that
both Jews and Gentiles are under the power of sin
(Rom 3:9) and equally need the salvation which
Jesus Christ has won for us in his death. Paul in
Romans was assuming that Jews need the Messiah,
and seeking to show that Gentiles too should be
evangelised. Today the boot is on the other foot.
We take it for granted that the Messiah or Christ is
for Gentiles, but may question whether Jews
should turn to him for salvation. The Bible is
realistic in its assessment. Both Jews and Gentiles
suffer the same problem of sin. And the one God
of all the world has provided in Jesus Christ the
one solution to that problem.

Some Christians can be somewhat naive in their
understanding of Jews. They think romantically
that all Jews still follow the Old Testament faith of
their fathers without any change or development.
They wonder why Jews today need the atoning
work of Jesus whereas Old Testament Jews could
be saved without knowing who the awaited Messiah
was. Actually of course Jews today not only believe
in the Bible, but also in the whole development of
rabbinic thought and particularly the Talmud.
Judaism is not just the faith of the Old Testament,

but has added much that is quite human. We have to agree with the rabbis in their very biblical understanding that failure to keep just one point of the law means that one has transgressed the whole (cf Jas 2:10)—all of us have done that!

With the passing of time attitudes are changing. An increasing number of Jewish and Gentile Christians are sharing the good news of the Messiah Jesus with Jewish neighbours and friends. It is now almost half a century since the Holocaust. Although the memory of this trauma will never be erased from Jewish minds, yet its bitterness begins to be softened as the years pass. To more and more Jews it is no longer a personal memory from their own experience. Only the middle-aged and old remember the nightmare. For them it is tragically hard to envisage faith in Jesus as the solution to the insecurity, bitterness and suspicion of other people which often follow the experience of persecution.

But as the Holocaust slips a little into history it has become more possible for some Orthodox Jews to face seriously the fact that Jesus is Jewish. Some searching books have been written, seeking to examine who he really was and how he fits into Jewish history. Many ordinary Jews around the world are more open today to consider the claims of Jesus if they are offered with sensitivity, loving friendship and relevance.

Who are the Jews?

The parliament or Knesset in Israel still debates the definition of a Jew. Legally, descent comes through the mother, not the father. But what rabbinic sanction must there be for a legal marriage? And can you be considered Jewish if you believe in Jesus as Messiah?

It is far from easy to define who is a Jew. And it is also true that there are many different sorts of Jews. There is no such thing as 'the typical Jew'. In China there are Chinese-looking Jews, in India and Sri Lanka there are brown-skinned Jews, the Falasha Jews from Ethiopia are black, European Jews are white. Traditionally Jews have been divided into two major groupings, Ashkenazim and Sephardim. The Ashkenazim lived in Christian lands, while the Sephardim were in Muslim and southern European countries. Their traditions and world-views differ enormously. But even within those two groupings huge differences exist. An American Jew may not see eye to eye with a French Jew, or a Yemeni with a Moroccan. Also Judaism consists not only of the Orthodox, but of various denominations. Large numbers of Jews again are not religiously practising, and some have assimilated, merging into the culture and language of the country where they live. So it is not easy in one short chapter to generalise about what God is doing among Jews.

Where do the eighteen million Jews live? Many assume that the majority will be in the state of Israel, but actually the three and a half million Israeli Jews are outnumbered by America's six million. Just the state of New York has about as many Jews as the state of Israel—is Brooklyn the new Zion? We do not know precisely how many Jews live in the Soviet Union, but estimates climb as high as four million—just imagine the problems if they all emigrated to the state of Israel! Already there are severe housing and social problems with just some tens of thousands coming to Israel. France plays host to some three quarters of a million, Britain a third of a million and then there are considerable communities in South Africa, New Zealand, Argentina and many other countries.

What about Jewish believers in Jesus?

Just ten or twenty years ago it was quite rare to meet a Jewish believer in Jesus. Today things have changed. In North America there are some fifty thousand Jewish believers, in Israel probably three thousand, in Britain several hundred as also in South Africa, France and elsewhere. Some have come to faith in Jesus through the vibrant personal witness of Gentile Christians, while others would never have received the gospel from a Gentile and have come to the Lord through other Jewish believers. But in one way and another God is building his church among the Jewish people.

Gentile churches

Scattered through Gentile churches and student Christian Unions in our various countries are quite a few Jewish Christians. In some cases a whole group is clustered in the one congregation and so are able to encourage one another, but generally these Jewish believers remain alone in being both Jewish and Christian. The obvious danger is that they sink anonymously into the prevailing Gentile context, thus losing their particular Jewish distinctives, their racial and cultural identity. This is sad for two reasons. Firstly the Jewish Christians miss out if they never manage to relate their Christian faith to their Jewish heritage. This can lead to a spiritually split personality—half Jewish and half Christian—where the two do not meet and become one. Secondly the Gentile churches miss out on all they could learn from a Jewish insight into the Scriptures and the Christian faith. By submerging their Jewishness, Jewish Christians rob the churches of much potential blessing. Happily, God is increasingly at work in this respect, for with the growing number of Jewish Christians in the churches they are beginning to stand up and be counted. But there are still many who confess that they have never told anyone in their church that they are Jews.

Messianic fellowships

Many people assume that you cannot be both a Jew and a Christian. I am often asked, 'When did you stop being a Jew?' My reply is always, 'When did you stop being English?' Thus the ecumenical dialogue group is called the Council of Christians and Jews on the assumption that the Christians will not be Jewish and the Jews will not be Christians.

It is a very important phenomenon in the history of evangelism among Jews that in these past few years a new movement has developed. New churches with a strong Jewish identity have sprung up not only in Israel, but also in many other countries. They are called Messianic Fellowships or Assemblies in some countries, Messianic Synagogues in America. Their existence, as strongly Jewish and yet also strongly Christian bodies, demonstrates clearly that it is after all possible to be both Jewish and Christian.

The Messianic Fellowships generally avoid vocabulary which is linked in Jewish minds to a history of persecution. Thus they do not call themselves churches, but fellowships or assemblies. The word 'Christian' is replaced by the term 'believer', while the concept of 'conversion', being often associated with forced conversions, is expressed in terms of 'becoming a believer'. Jewish believers within such fellowships generally prefer to call the Lord by the Hebrew name Yeshua ha—Meshiah rather than by the rather foreign title Jesus Christ.

The Messianic Fellowships are struggling to find forms of worship which reflect their Jewish culture and heritage. In this there is often a blend of the vivacious and lively together with the solemn and traditional. A lively more charismatic song with Israeli dancing may yield suddenly to an old Hebrew chant. What is merely vivacious can be superficial; what is only solemn may become boringly old-fashioned.

Inevitably there is also a tendency to see Scripture through Jewish eyes rather than by the traditional Gentile approaches. Equally Christian faith is applied to the issues which lie heavily on Jewish hearts and minds.

In fact, through these fellowships God is renewing a form of Christianity which in many ways is more culturally akin to the church of the New Testament period. They are looking at questions which faced new Jewish believers then, particularly in their relationship to the Old Testament Law and to the increasing presence of Gentiles in the church. And in these days much debate rages concerning the state of Israel.

As might be expected, considerable controversy

exists within the Christian church concerning these fellowships. Some observe the danger that they could become exclusive and separatist. Others note the possibility that they could stress their Jewishness more than their faith in Jesus as Messiah. A few feel threatened when they hear that traditional Gentile interpretations of the Bible and of theology can be questioned. It is of course true that these relatively new movements may yield sometimes to such temptations, but the New Testament churches were also not without their problems. Meanwhile we cannot but rejoice at the growing stream of Jews who are becoming believers in Jesus and are beginning to relate their faith to their Jewish heritage. This makes it easier for other Jews to follow them into faith in Christ. Surely God is at work—and yet it is still only a small minority of Jews who are coming to follow the Lord.

3
THE CHURCH'S GREATEST CHALLENGE
What is God doing among Muslims?

We have already noted that God controls not only the lives of his church and people, but also reigns as God over all the world, holding the reins of history in his sovereign hands. Under his direction the world of Islam has changed incredibly in these past twenty-five years. Our perception of Muslims has changed in two ways.

Firstly there is the significance for Muslims of the recent changes in East Europe. No longer is the West preoccupied with the communist world as its great rival. One can only ask whether the new division of power blocks will not be between Europe and America on the one side and the Muslim world on the other. Already one detects a sense of mutual fear and even hatred both among Muslims and Europeans. To many Muslims, Americans and Europeans are a satanic foe waiting for an opportunity to destroy Islam and its followers. Equally many westerners shudder at pictures of fanatical Muslim crowds surging through city streets, and think of Muslims as militant terrorists. Racial or religious caricatures of this nature always distort truth. They also work strongly against Christian love which is a necessary prerequisite for Christian witness. How can we share the good news of grace unless we are ourselves gracious in love?

A second change in our perception is based on economics. Just twenty-five years ago most people had never heard of the desert oases and little fishing villages of Kuwait, Bahrain or Dubai. The Muslim world was poor and backward with little significance in the wider arenas of world economics or politics. It is hard today to believe it. Muslims are convinced that it was God who used oil to demonstrate the truth and glory of Islam. Christians too believe that the revolutionising influence of oil was under God's sovereign control. What was his purpose? Was it to bring the two worlds of Islam and Christianity more closely together? Was it to give the church new openings for sharing the reality of God in Jesus Christ among Muslims?

Certainly it is true that the two worlds of Islam and the west have been drawn into close proximity both in western countries and in Muslim lands. Sadly they are often like oil and water—living next to each other, but without any vital relationship. Muslims in the west frequently form little ghettos apart from their white neighbours, often disliking and disliked. Likewise in Muslim countries westerners, drawn to work there by high salaries, are unable to make friendships with local people. Nevertheless the opportunity is there for Christians to observe Islam, and for Muslims to meet Christians. Because of this there is a small trickle of conversions both from Islam to

Christianity and vice versa. A few years ago it was almost unthinkable that Arab Muslims in the heartlands of Islam would become Christians. But now we begin to hear of family clans turning to Jesus Christ in one or two such countries and some leading individuals too who are being converted. In western countries there is a quiet flow of Muslims becoming Christians, particularly westernised second-generation young people. There is however no room for naive triumphalism in this, for it is still only a relatively very small number who are coming to faith in Christ. At the same time there is a corresponding trickle of westerners who have become disillusioned with what they have seen of Christianity and join Islam. But through the movements of history God has given Christians a new opportunity to show the beauty of God's grace in Christ to Muslims. Our lives will be seen and our words can be heard—what a challenge!

The church's response

'Please inform me of courses to help me to understand more about Islam and Christian witness among Muslims'; 'Please could you speak to our Christian Union about witness among Muslims?'; 'Please could you advise me what opportunities there would be for me in mission among Muslims?'. Over these past years it has been encouraging to receive many such letters from all over the world. It seems that God has been moving by his Spirit in the church worldwide to arouse a particular concern for mission among Muslims. At the college where I teach we have had various Korean and

Latin American students who have been called by the Lord to work in Muslim countries. Many African students too now have a deep call to such ministry. In Africa the churches are running various courses to train their workers for witness among Muslims. This may have developed partly because in the past Muslims and Christians spread their faiths largely among the tribes which still followed their traditional animistic religions. Now the buffer states of animism between the Christian and Muslim communities have largely been swallowed up by the two great world faiths. This means that Islam and Christianity confront each other directly.

In one way or another the Holy Spirit is challenging the church to be involved in witness among Muslims. Twenty years ago the church's big missionary concern was for the communist world. Today the world of Islam has captured Christians' attention for prayer and evangelism.

Witness among Muslims

In most Muslim countries it is illegal to witness to a Muslim and someone who is converted from Islam may well be killed. In such situations it is obviously singularly unwise to give any details concerning Christian mission in those lands. Unwise disclosure of information can lead to doors being closed for the gospel or to local Christians suffering severe persecution.

Muslims still shudder at the memory of the bitter Crusade wars between Christian and Muslim armies. They feel that the Christian crusading spirit was further evidenced in the long centuries of imperialism and colonialism in which Christian states dominated the world of Islam. Now in more recent years the presence of American and European forces in Muslim waters and even on the soil of the holy land of Saudi Arabia seems to many Muslims like a continuation of that history. In Muslim minds this is also linked to American support for the state of Israel which is anathema to Muslims. While many Christians see the hand of God at work in bringing the state of Israel to birth like a phoenix out of the ashes of the German gas chambers, Muslims see it as a Zionist and Christian plot against Islam.

Failing to understand Muslim sensitivities, some Christians talk and behave unwisely. Undiscerning support for Israel without any criticism of injustices against Palestinians does not reflect the character of the biblical prophets who demonstrated God's passion for holiness and justice. But it is equally wrong to join the critics of Israel in naive support of the Palestinians as if they were the purely innocent sufferers. Biblically God has laid down repentance as the precondition for the coming of his kingdom. There will be no godly peace, righteousness and justice in the Middle East until we see on both sides God's miraculous gift of humble repentance.

In the very sensitive context of Islam it is vital that Christians should be careful, humble and loving in their witness. Insensitive or triumphalistic power-consciousness will be unwise and counter-productive.

Both Jews and Muslims fear that Christian witness is aimed at undermining their community. It is particularly important therefore that new converts should be strongly encouraged to remain within their family and society. For this to be possible it may be necessary to develop patterns of Christian life and worship which are culturally related to a Muslim background. We are beginning to see this happen in some countries. For example in one South Asian Muslim area several thousand Muslims have become believers in Jesus as Lord and Saviour, but have remained in their former society. Their forms of worship look outwardly quite Muslim, but they have a clear biblical and Christ-centred faith.

Enormous challenges

1. North Africa

My wife and I were thrilled to visit the impressive ruins of many old churches in Tunisia. We saw where Augustine had preached in the fourth century, but some of the ruins were much earlier than that. The many huge churches witnessed to the great size of the Christian church in North Africa during those early centuries. But we sensed too the bitterness of the Christian church's defeat at the hands of the Muslim armies. Even the church buildings had been dismantled to provide building materials for new mosques. Today there are only some thirty indigenous Christians, not counting the few hundred foreign Protestant Christians and about 18,000 Roman Catholics living in Tunisia.[1]

Under the onslaughts of the Muslim armies and mass emigration, conversions to Islam and finally a terrible plague, the church gradually declined and died in North Africa west of Egypt. Islam stands triumphant and Christian witness is tough. The few Christian converts face tremendous pressure from their families, at work and in society. They are often imprisoned or hassled by the police. Over the years some have been poisoned or otherwise martyred for their faith. And yet today these little fellowships of local Christians are gradually growing—God is at work, although it is hardly revival.

2. *Turkic peoples*

All across Soviet Central Asia right into northern China live various peoples who speak languages related closely to Turkish. In the Soviet Union alone Islam claims some sixty million followers among these peoples. Until recently very little could be done to bring the gospel of Jesus Christ to them. But now the more open political situation in the Soviet Union has opened a door for more Christians from other countries to take professional jobs in those areas and quietly share the gospel. Local Russian Christians too are engaged in bold witness among Muslims. Bible translation and the production of Christian literature in local languages has begun. A few people are coming to faith in Jesus Christ.

Under Stalin many German communities from the Ukraine were forcibly moved into the remote and inhospitable areas where these Muslim peoples live. Many of the Germans were Christian and they formed their own churches. Sadly most of them were content merely to survive as Christians and had little vision for the evangelisation of their Muslim neighbours—and in the fearfully dark days of Stalinist oppression none of us can criticise them for this. Under Gorbachev greater freedom reigns and it would be easier for them to share their faith openly. But this same freedom also allows the Christians to move, and about a hundred thousand Christians have left the area, emigrating to Germany or Israel. While this has given new growth and impetus to the messianic fellowships of Israel, it has weakened the witness of the gospel in Central Asia.

3. The Middle East

If Saudi Arabia is the religious heart of Islam, Egypt is the intellectual centre. Because the prophet Muhammad was an Arab and the Qur'an was written in Arabic, the Arabs will always remain the key to the world of Islam. While Indonesia is the country with the largest number of Muslims and there are more Muslims in India, Pakistan or Bangladesh than in any Middle East country, nevertheless the bloodstreams of Islam flow out from Saudi Arabia, Egypt and the Middle East.

It would be an unwise prophet who sought to foretell the future of this turbulent area. It was early in 1990, just before Iraq's invasion of Kuwait, that the Pentagon stated that the Middle East was no longer in the centre of world attention. They said that Eastern Europe was now centre stage in the political and economic world, whereas the Middle East had lost significance! Just as the politics of the region bubble in a turmoil of uncertainty, so also it is hard to predict the future developments of Islam. Will fundamentalism win the day and bring in the fullness of Islamic law? Or will the divisions in the world of Islam cause some disillusionment? Might it be that somehow the rocklike fortress of Islam will begin to crack and yield converts in large numbers to Christian witness? There are at least some signs of a growing openness to read the Bible and in some countries a few people are finding their way to faith in Jesus Christ. But the fortress remains impressively strong.

4. The Indian sub-continent

India—100 million Muslims; Pakistan—100 million Muslims; Bangladesh—90 million Muslims; Afghanistan—10 million Muslims. In our concern for witness among Muslims we dare not overlook these huge populations. Pakistan and Bangladesh are moving steadily towards fuller implementation of Islamic law. If the fundamentalist rebels gain control of Afghanistan, they too want a rigid application of Islamic law to every area of life. Only Hindu India is relatively free from these pressures, although here too the Muslim population would like to have Muslim law for their own community and thus form almost a state within a state. Wherever Islamic law has power, it is particularly hard to communicate the Christian gospel. Witness to Muslims becomes strictly illegal and conversion from Islam to another religion can be punishable by death. The church will be marginalised and deprived of many of its rights. For example, it becomes very hard to obtain permission to build new churches and impossible to have any open witness.

But in each of these countries there is a growing interest among some Christians in sharing the gospel with their Muslim compatriots. Much new thinking is being done on how to witness among Muslims and what should be the forms of worship and church life among new converts. The result has been that some Muslims have begun to understand the gospel and hearing has led to faith.

5. *Europe and North America*

Multitudes of Muslims have come to live in North America and western Europe. This has caught the church by surprise and still today few church leaders have much idea how to help their members to relate to Muslim neighbours and witness to their faith. But over these past few years many helpful books have been written on this subject and a variety of courses and seminars have taken place to teach ordinary Christians at least the basics. Former missionaries overseas have returned to their home countries and become involved in witness here. And a growing number of local Christians have felt the call of the Lord to dedicate their lives to mission among Muslims.

Sadly the Salman Rushdie affair has deepened the chasm between the Muslim communities and their white neighbours. The Christian faith is largely linked in Muslim minds to the white community, so religion becomes a racial affair, which adds an unfortunate bitterness of feeling. But still some younger Muslims want to relate easily with the host culture. They make friends among local people, feel attracted to European ways and some become Christians.

Muslim societies in each of these different parts of the world present a huge and formidable barrier to the spread of the gospel. But God is quietly drawing a few to faith in Jesus Christ.

What means does God use to bring Muslims to salvation in Jesus Christ? Of primary importance is genuine, loving friendship. Personal relationships are of supreme significance in Muslim cultures, so it is vital that we develop long-term friendships. Then many Muslim converts have been moved by the reading of the Bible. Scripture distribution can play a vital role in witness among Muslims— Christians need to look for opportunities to lend or give the Bible or New Testament to Muslim friends. Muslims often believe strongly in dreams and visions. In his grace God meets us all in ways which fit our expectations and it is quite common to hear former Muslims testify of their conversion through a dream or vision. And then quite a few Muslims have found eternal life after experiencing a miraculous healing in the name of Jesus Christ.

The church—God's chosen instrument

In many Muslim lands Christian churches have survived long centuries of discrimination. Thus around fifteen per cent of the population of Egypt is Christian, largely belonging to the ancient Coptic Orthodox church which looks back to the apostle Mark as its founder. Five per cent of Jordan, eight per cent of Syria and three to four per cent of Iraq stand out as Christians in the midst of Muslim populations. Large numbers of Arabs and Palestinians in Israel and Lebanon are Christians. So too in Asia Christian churches live on as witnesses to Jesus Christ—many millions of Indonesians, seven or eight per cent of Malaysia, two per cent of Pakistan, a tiny half a per cent of Bangladesh and a mere handful of Christians in Afghanistan. In Muslim

Africa too Christian churches exist as potential beacons of light for their Muslim neighbours. We need to pray for our sisters and brothers in lands like Gambia, Senegal, Mali and Somalia.

In such Muslim situations it is easy for Christians to develop a sense of inferiority, aiming to survive rather than to witness and grow. Fear often replaces the joyful but humble boldness which should characterise Christians.

In country after country signs are emerging of a new life and vision among the ancient churches. Although mission from outside plays a vital role in witness, the key to evangelism is always in the national church. It is good to see growing numbers of foreign Christians taking jobs in Muslim countries with the specific aim of evangelism and of forming new Christian fellowships. More and more of these workers have been in their adopted countries long enough to have learned the language and culture well. They have also formed long-term friendships which allow a deeper and more personal sharing of the faith.

While we encourage and pray for these 'tent-makers', let us not forget the national churches.

4

A NEW HEART FOR THE CHRISTIAN CHURCH
What is God doing in Africa?

In terms of world faiths, the continent of Africa divides into different regions. North of the Sahara lie the strongly Muslim Arab countries which we have already briefly looked at in the previous chapter. South of the Sahara and halfway down Sudan the population moves from being Arabs to black Africans and Islam begins to yield to Christianity as the predominant religion. At first there is a mixture of faiths—half the population being Christian and half Muslim. But as we progress further south the different countries become increasingly Christian. Finally in southern Africa we find a belt of largely Christian nations. This includes the troubled but richly endowed land of South Africa where the majority black population is still ruled by the white minority and the injustices of the apartheid system fuel bitter resentment throughout the continent.

Maurice Sinclair in his book *Ripening Harvest, Gathering Storm* (MARC: 1988), shows the burgeoning growth of the Christian churches in the continent of Africa. Even including the strongly Muslim north he says that forty-four per cent of all Africans profess to be Christians. It used to be said that Christianity was so tied to imperialism and colonialism that with national independence the church would wither and perhaps die. The reverse has happened. Since the collapse of colonialism in the 1960s the church has mushroomed in sub-Saharan Africa. Strong and gifted church leaders have developed, evangelism and mission have flourished.

Sadly however the growth of the churches has not been matched by a corresponding social and economic development. In various countries drought has reduced the land to desert conditions, so that the Sahara has crept inexorably southwards. With the drought has come fearful famine, pictures of which have stirred the hearts and generosity of many of us as we have watched television. The ghastly tragedy of mass starvation is a deeply disturbing reality which makes the weight-conscious over-indulgent western societies appear a sick mockery. In these next years the west has got to find a way to share its food mountains with the starving.

Massive urbanisation plus the grave decline of African economies is causing degrading poverty. Slums with minimum or no sanitation sprawl around the edges of Africa's fast-growing cities and towns. Men have often gone to the cities in search of work and money, leaving their wives and children to tend the fields at home. This leads not only to the breakdown of family life with consequent moral problems, but also to a sense of hopelessness, under-development and poverty in country areas too.

In the light of such immense economic needs it is a double tragedy to see the continent torn by strife and war. Hard earned and desperately needed national resources are used to buy arms. Country after country has been devastated by one war after another. The formerly prosperous and educated Uganda was ruined in the struggles connected with Idi Amin. Drought-ridden Ethiopia and Sudan have suffered long years of bitter warfare. The horrendous bloodshed of Liberia's civil war defies description. South African apartheid has been closely connected with destructive wars in Namibia, Angola and Mozambique, as well as causing sad violence in South Africa itself and economic hardship in the neighbouring front-line states.

Now in more recent years a new scourge threatens to overwhelm black Africa—AIDS. In such countries as Zambia, Uganda, Rwanda and Zaire this has reached epidemic proportions, threatening to wipe out whole sections of the population. In recent satellite pictures of those areas the whole colouring has changed, for the forest has taken over where AIDS has depopulated whole villages. No longer is AIDS just the result of sexual promiscuity, for now it is so widespread that many children are born with the disease. Missionaries and the national churches are in the forefront of this desperate battle. So far it has to be said that their teaching on sexual morality has not borne much fruit, but ultimately this is the only way to check the spread of AIDS. Christians also lead the field in Africa in providing loving care for those who are slowly dying because of AIDS. In their fear and dire need many people are finding solace and new life in Christ and in fellowship within his church, but as Christians this does not soften the heartache as we 'weep with those who weep' (Rom 12:15) because of AIDS.

Optimism

Anyone who has spent time in black Africa will have sensed the amazing cheerful optimism and warm humour which generally characterises African cultures. The emotionally reserved and often negatively pessimistic European may view this positive and open-hearted approach as somewhat naive, but it contains a genuineness which shames the sophisticated facades of the west. We cannot but admire such optimism which persists despite the droughts, famines, poverty, injustice, wars and AIDS which we have just described.

This optimism is closely linked to an innate spirituality which underlies the whole worldview. Even outwardly-Marxist Africans in Angola or other countries generally retain a basic awareness of spiritual realities. While almost every African people has a traditional belief in a High God who is also creator of the world, in practice a whole host of lesser spirits has been added to supplement the often rather remote High God. Mother Earth, nature spirits and ancestral spirits abound in the African pantheon. In everyday life it is these spirits which can heal sickness, protect from curses and harm, help with the crops or enable a woman to have a baby. Even when people become Christians or Muslims they frequently revert to their traditional spirit practices when faced with sickness, death or other tragedies. But it is also this fundamental spirituality which makes so many Africans so receptive to the message of Jesus Christ.

African spirituality is usually expressed through dynamic music and dance. When visiting Africa I am always struck by the way even very young children seem naturally and spontaneously to dance to the music and clap in time with the syncopated beat. It is therefore interesting to note how many African churches have adapted quite traditional western hymns and given them a more African rhythm. Staid and unemotional worship hardly fits an African context, although traditional forms mean much to both Muslims and Christians.

African spiritual awareness is also often expressed by a clear and open relationship with God personally which leads to considerable prayerfulness. In the college where I teach we are often put to shame by our African students who may spend long hours in prayer each day while as Europeans we may struggle to have a regular half-hour devotional time. When one is in Africa relationship with God seems much less complicated and more natural. People also talk very freely and without embarrassment about God and about spiritual realities. God is so much a part of everything in daily life that it would be strange not to talk about him in normal conversation.

The church

It is always unwise to generalise about a whole continent as if there were no difference between the various countries. Actually of course each nation and each people is distinct. And there are enormous differences between West Africa and East Africa. History too has left an indelible mark. French, Portuguese, British, German, Belgian and Spanish colonialism each introduced different forms of education, politics and culture. While reaction against colonialism burns strongly, it still leaves behind an indelible heritage.

This is also true of the church. In French-speaking Africa the Roman Catholic church is often relatively strong while Protestantism may be very weak. But this is not always the case, for Zaire abounds with a multitude of Protestant churches of various types. In English-speaking countries Protestant churches are often very strong indeed. These will include the traditional denominations, but others may also have taken deep root. Thus the inter-denominational missions in many countries have formed strong churches which are now major African denominations. In East Africa the non-denominational Africa Inland Mission has brought to birth the Africa Inland Church, which in Kenya is as large as the Anglican church. In Ethiopia the Sudan Interior Mission has left behind a dynamic church which is the largest Protestant denomination in the country and has a vital witness in spite of fierce government persecution. In West Africa the Sudan Interior Mission and what was the Sudan United Mission can praise God for the large and dynamic churches they have brought into existence. Other missions too have played their part in God's missionary task of forming independent national churches which are strong in faith and witness.

But there is a danger. In spite of the fact that in

theory the various African churches are now indigenous and independent of foreign domination, in practice this is not always the case. The poverty of many African churches makes it easy for rich western churches to gain undue power through financial assistance. Money can easily have strings attached. The principal of one African theological college told me that he did not agree with the official teaching of his college on the second coming of Christ and on polygamy. When I remonstrated that he was the head of the whole college and presumably therefore had some say in these matters, he disagreed. If the college's sponsors in America discovered that the principal gave teaching which they did not approve of, they would withdraw support and the college would be bankrupt. Because of the dangers of such economic imperialism one African bishop said to me that western churches need to give much more sacrificially in order to find the Lord's blessing, but for the sake of the African churches it would be better if their money got lost before it arrived in Africa. True—and yet untrue! For the churches need help both in finance and in professional skills—in medicine, agriculture, education, Bible teaching and leadership training. The vital question is how western experts can assist the national churches and how financial aid can be given without paternalism and without gaining control over the development of the churches.

Revival

'Hello! I'm so happy to meet you. My name is Joseph and I was a fearful sinner and lost in my rebellion against the Lord. And then on 3 June 1983 I met

Jesus Christ and God saved me. Praise the Lord!'

I met Joseph when going for a walk one day and it was just a brief, casual encounter. The East African revival has influenced even everyday greetings and I had to learn to share a short testimony of that sort both before speaking or preaching and also when meeting people. This revival movement has been burning now for some sixty years and has deeply influenced the whole life of the churches in East Africa. It started and is still centred in the Anglican churches, but its vitality has spread more widely now. While at first it was not in any way related to the more recent charismatic movement, now it contains within itself both charismatic and non-charismatic tendencies. The chief characteristic of this burning movement of God's Spirit is a deep and open repentance. National Christians and missionaries alike have been moved to open confession of sin which has led to true reconciliation and often to humble, loving relationships.

As always with the work of the Holy Spirit weaknesses can easily undermine the beauties of God's working. Confession of sin can become just another traditional form. Christians can become proud of their confession and repentance. Renewed Christians can feel superior to other believers and disunity between charismatic and non-charismatic threatens the life of the whole renewal movement. And yet in his grace the Lord continues to overrule human sin and pride. The work of the life-giving Holy Spirit burns on.

In West Africa in more recent years a new evangelistic and missionary vision has broken into the churches. Already thirty years ago some churches joined together to initiate united evangelistic outreach not only to the followers of tribal religion, but also to their Muslim neighbours. This led to some churches growing significantly and a new enthusiasm capturing the hearts of many Christians. Just a few years ago a former student of the college where I teach formed a missionary society in the Nigerian churches to which he belonged. He has the vision of bringing the good news of Jesus Christ to those racial groups which previously had no Christian witness. His missionary society now has over six hundred active members, most of whom are witnessing in tribes in Nigeria itself but a few also work across the borders in other countries.

Throughout black Africa a multitude of new movements has mushroomed into existence. Generally these have been called 'Independency Churches'. Some of them resemble more traditional Protestant churches with beliefs which are largely in line with accepted Christian faith. Others are so closely akin to animistic tribal religion that other Christians cannot accept them as true churches. Most of them fall somewhere between those two ends of the spectrum. All of them are very African culturally. The majority have developed as splits from traditional Protestant churches, although a few have come out from the Roman Catholic church.

What has led to this multiplication of Independency Churches? Often they were started by a dynamic leader who had a life-changing spiritual experience, but found his charisma and leadership gifts were not given scope to be used in the traditional churches. He would perhaps notice that some aspect of teaching in the Bible was omitted or underplayed in that church. For example I visited an Independency Church where the leader felt the traditional churches failed to praise the Lord 'with loud clashing cymbals' (Ps 150:5) and so reacted against the whole westernised worship patterns of the church. The Independency Churches tend also to foster a strong sense of belonging. Like the vibrant music and the dynamic leadership model this also fits the African context. As Kenneth Kaunda of Zambia observes, 'Africa's gift to human culture must be in the sphere of human relationships.'[2] The theologian John Mbiti has noted the increasing breakdown of tribal communities and therefore has urged the church to become 'the new tribe'.

The Independency Churches often practise miraculous healing, spiritual gifts like tongues and exorcism of evil spirits. In this way they touch the deeper recesses of the African soul which are sometimes ignored by traditional churches which are too western in character. Unfortunately the fearful lack of adequate Bible teaching often allows unChristian excesses and almost animistic practices.

Conclusion

In general it has to be said that in most African churches there is a dearth of quality Bible teaching and theological undergirding. Many churches are financially poor with the temptation to become unduly dependent on the west. Professional skills are also in short supply. Despite all these weaknesses the large and fast-growing African church has so much to contribute to the mission of

God's church worldwide. All of us could benefit from their vitality, spontaneity of faith, spirituality, joyful humour and open-hearted personal relationships.

5

POLITICS AND CHURCH GROWTH

What is God doing in Latin America?

'Pray for the evangelical Christians of Latin America in these fearful days of persecution.' The call to prayer and commitment to share the gospel with Latin America came clearly to us at the theological college at which I was studying. In those days the few evangelical Christians of that continent suffered fierce opposition from the very traditional Roman Catholic church. Many pastors were martyred for their faith, churches were often burned down, Bibles were destroyed. The reforming influences of the second Vatican Council had not yet encouraged more enlightened views to spread through the Roman Catholic church.

Many years later a leader of the Bible Society in one country told me of his call to full-time service for Christ. His father and pastor had gone out to preach in a village, had been met by a Catholic mob and both men were stoned to death. At that time he had been just a boy, but had determined to continue the work begun by his father and pastor. I was impressed by his open-hearted lack of bitterness which now allowed him a generous warmth in relations with Roman Catholics.

If I had been told in those days that in the future I would visit and preach in huge Protestant churches in South America, I would have smiled disbelievingly. What a moving experience therefore to go to the enormous 'Brazil for Christ' church in Sao Paulo with its congregation at that time of 36,000 adults on a Sunday morning. In Chile too it was moving to attend a morning service with some 16,000 others in the Jotabeche Church in Santiago. In other cities too it was exciting to note the large congregations which have developed over the past twenty or thirty years.

Particularly in Brazil and Chile the mushrooming of Pentecostal churches has transformed the whole religious scene. Around 10 per cent of the total population of these two countries is Pentecostal. This has also made it much easier for other evangelical churches to gain a hearing and to grow.

Traditionally the Pentecostals in Latin America have largely flourished among the poor and uneducated. Their pastors are generally men who have earned their position by long years of successful ministry and church planting, not by academic theological training. In fact many of them have little biblical or theological teaching behind them. Indeed large numbers of Pentecostal pastors have very little schooling at all. Sadly their sermons sometimes reflect this and fail to satisfy the needs of the increasingly educated, upwardly mobile younger generation. While it is true that there is a growing number of middle class, more educated

Pentecostals throughout Latin America, it still remains the case that large numbers of more educated young people leave their churches. In fact, the Pentecostal churches are like a bath with both taps on full and the plug out! They are constantly gaining new members through their active street evangelism, but they also lose many. On balance, they win more than they lose, so the bath gets fuller and fuller.

The Roman Catholic church

In the early days of the Spanish and Portuguese conquests of Latin America the church went hand in hand with the colonial powers. The authorities not only ruled in secular matters, but they also held the spiritual power in their hands. In Paraguay the Jesuit priests functioned as a sort of state government with total authority over the lives of the Indians in their area. In fact the Jesuits even ran their own army and navy to defend their territory from invasion and their trade from foreign ships.

Inevitably this situation meant that the church was allied to the rich and powerful. To many it appeared to support the status quo and have little concern pastorally or socially for the poorer strata of society. However in more recent years a strong reaction to this has changed the character of the Roman Catholic church in the whole continent. Liberation theologians and ordinary priests have emphasised God's desire for justice. They have sided with the poor in the struggle to defeat oppression. These issues form the core of the life and thought of the Base Communities, smaller religious group meetings which allow for more discussion, informality and the affirmation of individuals' personal worth.

In the early days of the continent's conquest by the imperial powers, the indigenous peoples were generally forced into baptism, but the new religion of Roman Catholicism merely gave new names to the old divinities. Christianity formed a thin veneer over the earlier tribal religions. Today some church authorities are struggling to overcome this tradition of Christianised paganism by means of teaching through the Base Communities. In the Andean republics of Peru, Bolivia, Ecuador and Colombia attempts have been made to develop new systems of lay training together with an emphasis on Bible reading. While one applauds these efforts it has sadly to be noted that traditional religious roots run deep and are not so easily eradicated. Folk religion remains strong—and the Pope is not alone in encouraging it. The Pope on his visits worships particularly at local cult shrines. Many of the church's hierarchy also maintain this emphasis and now even some liberation theologians stress this aspect of the church's life.

The charismatic renewal has also sprung up in Latin American Catholic churches. While it tends to attract the middle classes and therefore to be politically and socially rather conservative, it has added spiritual warmth to traditional Catholic faith. With some Catholic charismatics a new Christ-centred and biblical approach has evolved, but with others it has merely added a heartfelt vitality to the old forms and beliefs of folk catholicism.

Protestants

As we have already noted, the largest movement in the continent is that of the Pentecostals, but they are not the only churches which show significant growth these days. Some of the churches founded by inter-denominational missions are now large and influential. Thus in Peru the Peruvian Evangelical Church has almost 50,000 members and its people sometimes play significant parts even in the world of politics. In the huge land of Brazil with its population of around 150 million a multitude of different Pentecostal and other Protestant churches flourish. In the context of openly spiritistic movements and animistic practices which came with slavery from Africa it is not surprising that more charismatic churches do well. They deal specifically with the demonic backgrounds of those who come to them. The leader of one such church reminded me that western Christians often have an inadequate doctrine of conversion. He rightly pointed out that in conversion we turn not only from sin to Christ and his righteousness. We also turn from Satan. In baptism too we renounce not only the works of Satan, but also Satan himself and therefore all previous links with demonic forces. This emphasis makes the Pentecostal and charismatic churches particularly relevant to the Brazilian situation.

While the Assemblies of God Pentecostals are clearly the largest denomination in Brazil with at least five million members, the anti-charismatic Baptists also flourish. They open a new church somewhere in Brazil every week. They now have over 650,000 members and continue to grow.

While the Pentecostals are often very weak indeed in the content of their teaching, the Baptists have developed a string of Bible schools and strongly emphasise good biblical teaching. Their Bible schools are not only for training future pastors and full-time workers, but also often include night classes for ordinary Christians after work.

Living in the middle between other Protestants and the Roman Catholics there is the Anglican church. In a strange way it is able to relate to all and also to serve all with its non-residential Bible courses. These are used widely by a rich variety of churches. Although the Anglican church is still quite small, it is growing rapidly in some countries.

Under the shadow of the north

Geography should never be forgotten. The countries of Latin America cannot ignore the fact that immediately to their north lies the great economic and spiritual power of the USA. North America dominates the economies of her poorer neighbours to the south. Culturally too the influence of the United States cannot be ignored. Likewise multitudes of missionaries pour south to bring not only the central message of Jesus Christ, but also their particular denominations, doctrinal distinctives, evangelistic methods and finances. This leads to a love–hate relationship in which things American are admired and copied, but in many people there festers some resentment.

In the summer holidays crowds of young Americans come south to gain experience and serve the Lord while enjoying a short break from their studies. Such short-term mission experience can change their whole outlook on life and in some cases leads on to a commitment to long-term mission work. At the same time there is a real danger that large numbers of naive and inexperienced youngsters may underline an impression that evangelical churches are pawns of North America, which could cause some resentment among local Christians. This is of course true in many parts of the world, not just Latin America.

The dominating wealth of the United States is sometimes seen also in the missionaries whose homes and life-styles may be very different from those of the people they serve. In one city a mission leader who was struggling with this problem took me on a tour of the city. We went from one mission property to the next in prime sites. At each place he told me the commercial value of the property, which ranged from half a million to one million dollars. No wonder national churches cast covetous eyes on mission finances and sometimes demand the handover of their properties to the local Christians.

Injustice

Our television sets have brought before our eyes the crying needs of the poor in Latin America. I remember visiting a family in a pathetic shack in Sao Paulo, Brazil and looking out from their door at the extreme wealth of the business sector just a few hundred yards down the road. In Lima, Peru the dreary shanty town areas stretch for mile after mile on the desert sand outside the city. The squalor of some such districts contrasts sharply with the luxurious wealth of the middle classes.

But it is not only the newly urbanised poor who suffer the poverties and indignities of an unjust system. In the countryside and villages the peasants live at the mercy of their landowners. Debt makes them almost slaves to the rich. There often seems no escape from the calamity of poverty and debt when your land and labour are in pawn.

We have seen already that some Roman Catholics have taken up the political cudgels on behalf of the oppressed. Liberation theologians have brought this injustice to the attention of the church worldwide and of the media. Many ordinary priests and nuns actually live in the shanty towns among the poor in order to serve in a very practical way.

The Pentecostals usually claim that they are apolitical and refuse to get involved in such questions. But in a different way they too have a ministry related to the poor, for most of their membership comes from such circles. Their emphasis on miraculous healing meets a particular need among people who cannot afford to go to a doctor. Socially the outcast poor find self-worth and esteem in churches where they are called 'brother' or 'sister', where they can get up and give a testimony and everyone joins in giving glory to God for them and embraces them. In the Pentecostal churches they feel they have importance as people.

Although most Pentecostal churches avoid all involvement in politics, it sometimes happens that politicians woo their support in elections. In Chile and Brazil particularly, the Pentecostals form such a significant proportion of the electorate that election candidates promise electricity, drains, better water supplies or other benefits for the shanty areas in order to win votes.

In non-Pentecostal churches and missions there has been considerable emphasis on social ministries to help the poor. This has not only meant the distribution of food and clothing, medical care and schools, but also the establishing of some cottage industries to give employment and training in work skills. I still use some beautiful leather coasters bought from just such a cottage industry in Lima.

Evangelicals in Peru have played a formative part in the writing of the national constitution and indeed in the attempt to ensure justice and honesty in the political process. In Central America evangelicals have taken the lead in party politics and sometimes have gained high office, but there has been a danger that they have been unduly right-wing in their views and too much under the dominant influence of the United States.

Many people feel that the day of extreme left-wing or right-wing dictatorships has passed in the continent of Latin America. There seems to be a movement towards more democratic forms of government. The question of justice and greater equality both of wealth and of opportunity still hangs like a dark cloud over this part of the world. Political, social and economic changes are on the way. What role will the churches play in the process?

Will the Roman Catholic church shake off the dominant influence of superstitious folk religion and allow a renewal of biblical and Christ-centred faith? Will the mushrooming Pentecostals lose their way because of their inadequate Bible teaching? Or will they move increasingly out from among the very poor and uneducated, following the social mobility which allows their young people to move more into the middle classes and gain education? Will the fast-growing evangelical churches of Central America become the primary religious forces of their countries? And will they in South America also continue to grow rapidly and spread out into all strata of society with the gospel of Jesus Christ?

Latin America is an exciting continent.

6

COLOURFUL CROWDS IN A CONTINENT OF DIFFERENCES

God's work in Asia

Christians commonly emphasise how Jesus Christ related to individuals in a very personal way. Less often do we take note of the fact that he also had compassion for the crowds, for example in Matthew 9:36, as he moved among the throngs of people in Israel.

I remember how small I felt standing in the middle of a huge new housing area in Singapore for the first time. Tens of thousands of people swirled round and past me as I looked up at the blocks of flats stretching into the sky. Does Jesus Christ also love the crowded cities of Asia with their population of millions jammed into relatively small areas? Or does he only care for individual families in more spacious suburbs and individuals in rural villages and tribal areas?

Of course Asia does still have tribal groups which need the good news of Christ. Vast numbers of people are scattered in huge rural areas with innumerable villages which hardly find a place on the map. But more and more the multitudes drift into immense cities like Jakarta, Manila, Bangkok, Tokyo, Bombay, Calcutta and many others. When surrounded by the awesome multitudes of Asia we need to remind ourselves that our Lord related, and still relates, to crowds as well as individuals.

Most Europeans fail to appreciate the immense size of Asian populations. China alone has some eleven hundred million people—considerably more than all Africa and Latin America put together. India has a further eight hundred million; Bangladesh over a hundred million; Pakistan a hundred million. In East Asia, Indonesia has about 185 million—as many as Britain, France, Holland and Spain together. Then the little islands of Japan bulge to overflowing with more than 120 million. Asia houses at least half the people for whom Christ died.

Different histories

The silk trade of China and Japan, the spices of Indonesia, the rubber and tin of Malaysia, the romance of the orient generally—it's no wonder that Europeans were drawn to Asia like bees to honey. The Portuguese conquered large areas, but finally were pushed back to the tiny enclaves of Macao on the coast of China, Goa in India and half the island of Timor in Indonesia. The Danes found their way to India, but did not penetrate beyond that. The Dutch battled with the Portuguese and ended up victorious in Indonesia where they ruled for over three hundred years. The French carved a niche for themselves in Indochina—Vietnam, Cambodia and Laos. The Americans arrived late on the scene, defeated the Spanish and enjoyed half a century's colonialism in the Philippines until independence was granted in 1946. The British ruled in the Indian sub-continent and under the genius of Sir Stamford Raffles developed the great city state and port of Singapore. Before that Penang and Malacca in Malaysia ruled the spice trade from the eastern islands of Indonesia. The British also won a toe-hold into China with the acquisition of Hong Kong. Perhaps we should note too that for three years they held power in Indonesia during the Napoleonic wars, leaving a lasting mark on that great country—they still drive on the left and it was under the British that missionary work among Muslims was first permitted there.

The differing colonial backgrounds have left behind a rich variety of economic, educational, political and even cultural systems. Of course not all Asia submitted to foreign domination, for Thailand and Japan remained independent throughout the history of imperialism. Korea never came under western powers, but suffered under Japanese rule from 1910 until the end of the Second World War in 1945.

The various countries of Asia differ not only because of their varied histories in relation to colonialism. They are also very different racially and therefore culturally and religiously.

While the vast bulk of China overhangs all the rest of Asia and sends its people into all lands, the indigenous peoples of the surrounding countries vary considerably. In Korea and Japan Chinese philosophy and religion have deeply influenced the whole evolution of culture, so it is not only the writing in these three societies which is similar. Culturally, however, Japanese, Koreans and Chinese also have marked differences between them. The Thai have intermarried a great deal with Chinese, so that many leading families in Thailand have at least some Chinese blood in their background. Again the Thai are markedly different from the Chinese, but Chinese influences stand out clearly. During the Vietnam war it was often assumed by western observers that the peoples of Indochina were fundamentally one. This was far from the truth. While the Lao relate closely in culture to the Thai, the much more dynamic Vietnamese are of different stock. Cambodians on the other hand look back with pride to the ancient Khmer kingdom and empire of which they were the centre. The Khmer not only stem from totally different roots from the Lao or Vietnamese, but their historic national pride would not permit them to submit to the domination of another race. Utterly different in every way from all the above peoples are the Malay races of Indonesia, Malaysia and the Philippines.

In religion too we may observe vast differences between the different countries and peoples of Asia. All the major world faiths are strong here. Islam dominates in South East Asia among the Malay peoples and is the official religion of Malaysia, the predominant faith in Indonesia and the distinctive flag of rebellion against the majority Roman Catholic Philippines in the south of that country. Theravada Buddhism, the stricter form of that religion, reigns in Thailand, Laos, Burma and Sri Lanka, while Mahayana Buddhism and Confucianism join hands with Shinto in Japan, with traditional Korean shamanism in Korea and with Taoism among the Chinese. While Nepal is the world's only Hindu kingdom, the majority of Indians follow the various streams of Hindu religion. Just as the Chinese have migrated all over Asia, so too have the Indians and they have carried with them their Hindu faith. In the melting-pot of Asia mosques rub shoulders with Hindu and Buddhist temples. And they all vie for the souls of the relatively small tribal groups which still cling to their traditional forms of religion. In some cities little pockets of Jews can also be found.

This is the variegated context in which the Christian church lives and witnesses.

The church

Not surprisingly, it is impossible to generalise about the Christian church in Asia. In some countries it is large and strong while in other areas the casual visitor would hardly notice that the church exists. Various expressions of the Christian faith manifest themselves in the different lands of Asia—charismatic, non-charismatic, Anglican, Reformed, Pentecostal and a host of other denominations.

1. Strong churches

There are two East Asian countries which possess large and growing churches apart from the Roman Catholic nation of the Philippines. In South Korea and Indonesia the church flourishes and forms a significant part of the total population—in Korea about twenty-five per cent and in Indonesia perhaps about twenty to twenty-two per cent. In

Indonesia no one knows the accurate statistic, for the pressures of Islam encourage both the government and the churches to downplay the size and growth of the Christian church.

Until relatively recently South Korea's predominant Buddhism held little attraction for large portions of the population. Korea's rapid development economically and in education outpaced the thinking and practice of Buddhism, which seemed to many a mere relic of the past. This meant that it presented little opposition to the rapid growth of the church in its dynamic witness. In more recent years however Buddhism has begun to make considerable strides in its adjustment to the modern world. Today one can even see well-educated Buddhist monks wearing more modern styles of their traditional monks' clothing.

In the early years of mission work among the Koreans, great emphasis was given to indigenous structures of self-support, self-government and self-propagation. The American missionary Nevius pioneered this approach. The Korean churches today take it for granted that they are totally independent of any foreign domination. Of course their financial wealth helps them to remain free from economic strings manipulated from the west.

The Korean churches have developed a thoroughly Korean character which makes it much easier for local people to join them. While the scandal of the cross of Christ may remain, few cultural barriers hinder Koreans from conversion to the Lord and membership of the church. In some ways it is not always easy to see what is genuinely biblical Christian faith and what is just an adaptation of traditional non-Christian Korean ways. For example western Christians are always deeply impressed by the emphasis there on prayer. The capital city Seoul witnesses traffic jams as people crowd into the early morning prayer meetings. Many pastors will have a couple of days of prayer alone on the 'prayer mountains' before they preach on the Sunday. Korean Christians give the rest of us a tremendous challenge in their practice of heartfelt and believing prayer. But it has to be said that in traditional non-Christian Korean religion it was believed that the longer one prayed, the more likely you were to get the answer. Generally I have little doubt that Christian prayer in Korea stems from a deep trust in the Lord and dedication to him, but there could just be some whose practice of prayer retains the superstitious character of pre-Christian beliefs.

In the early days of Korean Christianity, and particularly under the Japanese occupation, the Christians knew what it was to suffer for their faith. And the church was known to stand for Korean national rights. The martyrdom of some pastors and other Christians has opened the door for witness today.

I well remember one evening sitting in a restaurant high above the great city of Seoul as darkness fell and the city lights began to twinkle. What an amazing sight! Hundreds of neon-light crosses stood out in the midst of all the lights. Each of those crosses represented a Reformed church, most of them with large congregations. When talking about Korea, most western Christians think immediately of the huge Pentecostal church founded and led by Paul Yonggi Cho which is the largest church in the world. When visiting I tried to count, and reckoned that some 250,000 people attended the various halls in the services that Sunday. In fact even more Korean Christians throng into the Reformed Presbyterian churches with their total membership of about six and a half million.

The Korean church has been moved by the challenge to world mission. A variety of indigenous missions have sprung up and Korean missionaries are fanning out into all the world with the good news of Jesus Christ. Many have a particular concern for the Muslim world. While mission training is being done in Korea, help is needed in this. Few Koreans have mission experience of any depth to pass on to those in training.

In Indonesia too the church has grown remarkably. Unlike Korea, however, the Christian church in Indonesia goes back a long way in history. Already in 1611 some 100,000 people had turned to Christ. Since then the gospel has reached out to most of the islands off this huge archipelago. The spread, however, is uneven. In North Sumatra and Sulawesi whole races have become Christian—for example the Toba Bataks, with some four million people, are a wholly Christian group. On the other hand Islam reigns supreme among many other peoples. Thus the Acheh people in the very north of Sumatra follow Islamic law with a rock-like adherence to the faith of Islam. Between these two extremes lie the gentle Javanese, the largest race in Indonesia, some of whom follow Christ while the majority still adhere to Islam.

Most Indonesian Christians belong to the traditional Reformed churches and the Batak Lutherans. But more recently a multitude of new denominations and movements have come into Indonesia from overseas and yet others have sprung up as new indigenous Indonesian Christian groups. While the external forms of the traditional churches appear quite Dutch because Indonesia was first evangelised by Dutch missions, in fact these forms have taken deep root in Indonesia during the past three hundred years and now appear natural to the Indonesian scene.

The exceedingly rapid growth of the church inevitably produces a need for Bible teaching and training at every level in the church. Many large churches exist outside the cities with little trained leadership and with inadequate teaching. Ordained ministers can sometimes be overwhelmed with their responsibility for several large congregations, so that they churn out baptisms, Lord's Suppers and weddings like sacramental sausage-machines. Our experience in the Indonesian churches is of a very real hunger for genuine spiritual vitality and for living exposition of the Bible and Christian truth. Christians cry out for training for youth work, Sunday School teachers, church-planting evangelists and Bible teachers for home groups, rural congregations and baptismal preparation classes.

When presented with the facts of very fast church growth it is easy to respond with a glad 'Hallelujah'. There is indeed much for which to praise God, but honesty compels us also to face the reality of the weaknesses and needs of the churches.

2. Unresponsive areas

Asia is a continent of contrasts. The ebullient and mushrooming churches of Korea and Indonesia seem far removed from Japan or Thailand, where the Protestant churches have only 0.5 per cent of the population and every new convert to Christ represents a hard-won triumph of grace.

In Japan not only do materialism and the immense pressures of a hard-working society stand against commitment to Christ, but there is further resistance from traditional community values and particularly the practice of ancestor veneration. When a young person adventures beyond conventional boundaries and perhaps becomes a Christian, this may be tolerated, but it is assumed that they will revert to ancestral practices and traditional religion and life when they marry. Backsliding therefore becomes normal for many, so churches generally remain small.

Many country areas remain unevangelised or strongly resistant to the introduction of the Christian faith, and even large towns and cities will only have a few small churches shining as dim lights in the prevailing darkness. Whole areas of cities may continue without any Christian presence.

Yet the picture of gloom still has a silver lining. Because of their over-population and their economic success, the Japanese spread out from their islands into all the world. Parallel to this the churches have also developed a worldwide missionary vision. Together with many Koreans and Chinese the Japanese too are sending increasing numbers of missionaries into other countries, including the tough mission work of the Muslim world.

In Thailand, Theravada Buddhism, the stricter form of that religion, mixes with an animistic cult of the spirits to hold the people in bondage. To be Thai is to be Buddhist. The Christian churches can easily be seen as a foreign intrusion into Thai life. The apparently easy-going friendly tolerance is hard to penetrate with a message of absolute and unique truth in the one Saviour Jesus Christ. Christian witnesses feel like boxers punching a glutinous jelly. It yields politely, gently envelops the intruding fist and quietly returns to its former shape.

Behind the smiling veneer of Thai Buddhism hide very real problems. With the notable exception of the Philippines, Thailand is reckoned to have more inter-personal violence than any other Asian country. While Buddhiṣm aims to repress all emotion in its struggle to lose self-awareness, actually it is like a boiling kettle without any outlet for the steam. The peaceful exterior eventually explodes in violence. Sexual immorality and a massive prostitution problem bring untold heart-ache. In more recent years fearful poverty has increased in some areas. Buddhism lacks social solutions to these problems. Despite some excellent Christian ministry among prostitutes, thus far the Christian churches have not yet gained a name for offering more satisfactory answers to the nation's needs.

3. Between the extremes

Many Asian countries have neither huge nor min-iscule Christian communities, but somewhere between those two extremes. Thus in Malaysia some seven and a half per cent of the people belong to the churches, of which the largest among the Protestants are the tribal churches of East Malaysia and the Methodists. While about half the population is Malay racially and Muslim religiously, the churches grow among the Chinese, Indians and tribal peoples. It has been a special privilege to my wife and myself to witness the steady growth of these churches. When we lived in Malaysia back in the 1960s we knew many churches with only fifty or a hundred members, but most of these now welcome congregations of two or three hundred active believers. Many have become mature spiritual leaders of high calibre.

Still, much remains to be achieved. Large numbers of Chinese Buddhists and Indian Hindus still have little opportunity to hear the gospel. Christians tremble at the thought of sharing their faith with Muslims, because it is illegal. Christian books on evangelism are banned, and Christians have been imprisoned and even tortured for being involved in witness among Malay Muslims. While some Christians remain determined to share their faith freely but wisely with all people, others have been frightened into silence.

In the Philippines, Protestant churches flourish, but not to the extent of Indonesia or Korea. Rather over ten per cent of the sixty million population belong to Protestant churches, which at present are growing rapidly. Sadly however the easy-going Philippino culture, reacting with the influx of a wide variety of independent missionaries, has led to an almost ludicrous multiplication of denominations. For example some three hundred Baptist denominations vie with each other—and the constant splitting of Pentecostal churches defies statistical research. Somehow in the midst of this unseemly disunity the Lord still works. As in other Asian countries God has developed mature spiritual leaders for his church as well as many dynamic spiritually-minded Christians.

Church and society

The social needs of the continent are immense and the church responds to this. Churches are involved in ministry among Taiwan's factory workers in their vast blocks of flats resembling the conditions of battery hens. In Hong Kong Christians have pioneered work among drug addicts and those trapped in industrial sweated labour. Liberating evangelism saves some prostitutes from sexual slavery in Thailand. In Malaysia the indigenous mission Malaysian Care has various residential homes to help children in need, ex-prisoners, prostitutes and other needy people. To some extent Asia's evangelism does go hand in hand with social action.

China

Some years ago I belonged to a rather liberal Christian group for the study of Maoism and Communist China. In those days any reference to Christians and the church was derided as irrelevant to modern China. Critics thought that only a few old ladies still clung to old-fashioned bourgeois ideas of religion. How wrong they were! When Mao died and more accurate news of the church trickled out from behind the bamboo curtain, we realised that God had kept his people in triumphant and enduring faith. Indeed the churches had multiplied.

We can only guess how many Christians there

are now in China. Some cite figures as high as a hundred million, while others estimate a mere four million. Between those two extremes most China-watchers consider about fifty million a reasonable guess. In any case we know that the relatively small churches of 1948 have mushroomed despite the years of fierce persecution and militant atheism.

Throughout the dark years of persecution the government allowed the official church to remain in compromised political subservience. In this way the authorities presented a picture of freedom to visiting dignitaries from overseas. Today those churches live much more freely and can preach with fewer restraints. Increasing numbers flock into their services. Yet perhaps the greatest growth has come in the independent house churches. For British readers we need to point out that these have little in common with what we call 'House Churches', for the Chinese independent churches may often be non-charismatic. These congregations rejected all compromise with the state and refused to allow any government interference in the choice of leaders, the content of their preaching or in the forms of their meetings. As a result they suffered particularly ferocious persecution. Martyrdom and prison threatened them for years.

Before the tragic events of Tiananmen Square life had become somewhat easier for the churches, but then the government cracked down again and Christians began to suffer once more. Gradually now the thumb-screws are being eased, but presumably the nation's leaders are well aware that Eastern Europe's revolutions found their focal point in the church. They will surely therefore keep a watchful eye on the church lest the same should happen in China.

What happens in the immense land of China cannot but overflow and influence other areas of Asia. The miracle of the church's enduring faith and growth in China should encourage us all. When China really opens to the outside world, its church will play a major role in mission to other countries. Meanwhile the door for expatriate workers has opened into China and increasing numbers of Christians teach English or do other jobs there. Their witness in China's current spiritual vacuum can be significant and it may encourage the national churches. But foreigners will need to be humble and patient, not rushing into China with our own plans and ideas. We need to work sensitively in co-operation with local Christian leaders and under their direction. Gradually we may be sufficiently accepted to be able to help with the Bible teaching, training and literature production which are much needed.

Conclusion

These few sample situations provide a taste of the sheer size and multi-faceted diversity of Asia.

7

THE BIGGEST CHURCH OF THEM ALL
God's work in North America

Skyscrapers dominated the skyline on a brightly coloured postcard produced by a Christian mission in the United States. Beneath the array of imposing buildings stood the slogan 'Every little village dreams of becoming a major city'. My thoughts went back to the Hertfordshire village where we live. Did people there dream of Stanstead Abbotts one day becoming a huge city with all its wealth, traffic, crowds of people and towering office blocks? Our village might consider this more of a nightmare than a dream.

But of course it remains true that success will produce growth. Churches which demonstrate the vital life of Christ will attract new people into their congregations. If people come to life in Christ and are brought into the church, then inevitably that church will become larger. This very obvious principle applies equally to mission societies. If they attract new recruits they cannot remain small. Growth in numbers does indicate an inner vitality which draws new members into fellowship. The growth of the New Testament church provides a clear example of this. As Europeans we must be careful not to despise the American dream of dynamic growth. The slogan 'small is beautiful' may merely justify stagnation and lack of vision.

What image does the expression 'American Christianity' conjure up in the average European's mind? We shall probably think immediately of the scandals of television evangelists. We are all aware of the dangers of huge wealth, media glamour and considerable popular influence. Right back in Old Testament times God continually warned his people of the twin temptations of sex and money. Christians today still need to heed those warnings. European television has enjoyed the unseemly pictures of American television evangelists confessing their sexual sins with public tears. The superficial glamour of their tinsel world places dark question marks over their repentance and indeed over the sincerity of their gospel preaching. Such suspicions apply equally to the huge American drive-in churches, crystal cathedrals and slickly professional church services where beautifully trained choirs produce their songs like automatic machines dispensing cans of Pepsi Cola.

But is all this really representative of American Christianity? Of course such aberrations do form one aspect of the whole, but there is much more. It has been said that American history has produced an emphasis on freedom and democracy. The founding fathers escaped from British persecution which demanded monochrome conformity. Then the pioneering movement westwards across the vast unexplored continent led to a spirit of independence and adventurous initiative. This encourages everything and everybody to develop to their full potential. It is true that sin and heresy can flourish, so that we are shocked by gross immorality among some well-known Christian personalities and by the mushrooming of every imaginable sect and heresy. But we must not ignore the parallel reality of good things which also multiply and flourish. Success stories abound in American churches and missions. Again and again we are regaled with tales of American churches which have grown from nothing to massive congregations with thousands of active members in just a very few years. New dynamic missions spring up to evangelise the world and to reach out to areas and peoples where the gospel was largely unknown. Major movements like Youth with a Mission and Operation Mobilisation stem from American roots. Influential new thinking on mission produces renewed vision and relevant strategies for local evangelism, church leadership and structures, and worldwide mission.

In a recent visit to a major Central Asian city in a previously closed area of the world I found some thirty-five foreign Christian workers. It did not surprise me to discover that virtually all of them came from the United States. They have a pioneering dynamic which inspires them to find ways to push open new doors for mission. It is true that our American friends sometimes trample over national sensitivities with a naive lack of wisdom. They are sometimes even worse than the British at learning languages and adjusting to other cultures, but their warmhearted confidence and friendliness often compensate for such failures. While

European missionaries may demonstrate wisdom and cultural sensitivity in their work under the direction of local Christian leadership, the pioneering spirit of American missionaries gets the job done. We proudly feel that they have much to learn from us, but we desperately need some of their enthusiasm, zeal and drive.

The church in North America represents a vast array of large denominations and movements, independent churches and para-church organisations. Such a huge and variegated church defies any brief descriptions which can only oversimplify in their generalisations. It is estimated that well over forty per cent of the total population of the United States regularly attend church. This means that the American church contains about a hundred million Christians, whereas British churches attract a mere four million. According to Patrick Johnstone's *Operation World* the Southern Baptist Convention alone has over fourteen million members and all the various Baptist denominations together have a membership of around twenty-seven million. Such statistics show how tiny European churches actually are, and compel us to realise the influence which the American churches wield in the Christian church and in mission worldwide.

European Christians may feel somewhat uncomfortable with the rather traditional right-wing Christian culture of the 'Bible belt' in the southern states of the USA. We may be critical of the fact that most such churches have little concern for racial or economic justice, so that wealthy middle-class white churches stand in marked contrast to shabby black churches nearby. In some cases

Christianity may represent a cultural package rather than a dynamic commitment to the living Christ. Many may adhere to an established set of doctrines with an attendant list of 'do's' and 'don'ts' which can replace a real study and knowledge of the Bible. Despite all the weaknesses of Bible Belt Christianity these churches do lobby for moral decency in society, fighting against the inroads of pornography, media violence and widespread abortion. They also give sacrificially for the work of mission worldwide and send large numbers of missionaries overseas.

In former years when the pioneer American settlers began to move west across the continent, the more traditional churches tended to remain comfortably in their east coast buildings. Sadly they frequently lacked the vision to follow the rugged pioneers as they opened up the huge new territories across America to the Pacific Ocean. As a result Christians gathered in free and independent churches in the central and western states. While in Europe it is the mainline denominations which still represent the majority of the church-going population, in America free and independent churches attract large numbers. In Europe the ecumenical World Council of Churches is influential, but in America less than half the churches owe any allegiance to it. In Europe evangelical Christians form a minority of the total church, while in America they are the majority.

As we have already noted, the church in America contains a rich variety of movements. There is not only a multitude of denominations, but also churches among many different races. Immigrants of many nations from all over the world have come to the United States in search of a new life and together they have built a society of incredible diversity. Millions of Hispanics, blacks, Koreans, Chinese and Italians rub shoulders with the largest and most influential Jewish community in the world, and there are also whites from all over Europe. Missionaries from relatively remote tribal areas overseas sometimes return to America to find more people from that tribe in California than in the country of their origin. A whole variety of ethnic churches has emerged, such as Jewish messianic synagogues, Chinese, Japanese and Korean churches. Black churches in America have begun to send their people back to West Africa as missionaries, although they quickly discover that their black American culture differs radically from that of West Africa. This is equally true of Korean, Chinese and Japanese Americans wishing to return to their mother countries. In the search for our roots we sometimes forget that very different plants have grown up in the soil of another country. Nevertheless these ethnic churches are developing a new potential for worldwide Christian mission.

A tradition has evolved in North America for many young people to study for a year or two in a Bible school after graduating from high school. As a result huge Bible schools have trained a multitude of Christians for service in their local churches or for wider mission. Crowds of these young students will travel overseas for their vacations for a short spell of work with a mission, particularly in the neighbouring continent of Latin America. It may be debatable just how much use such short-term workers may be for the churches and in evangelism in Latin America, but there can be no doubt that a proportion catch the vision for overseas mission and will later return long-term. In the American churches too the Bible schools provide a reservoir of workers with more knowledge of their faith and the Bible. While the Bible schools may attract thousands of students onto their immense campuses, the graduate study seminaries provide more exacting studies for smaller numbers of young people who have their sights set on full-time ministry. As in most other countries, these training establishments have significant influence on the character of American church life and theology. Some of them have adventurous programmes of study which provide a thorough but open-hearted training. Others have a rigid and doctrinaire approach which forces students into a particular theological line and does not permit any divergence from what is taught. American seminaries and Bible schools range from a very high quality to quite a low academic level, although sometimes even the schools of lesser reputation may still grace their graduates with BA and MA degrees.

The rather independent and democratic character of American life also influences the American approach to education and the media. Whereas in Britain Christians are urged to get involved in secular television and radio in order to introduce a more Christian influence into these very strategic means of communication, in America the emphasis lies rather on forming specific Christian stations. Likewise British Christians have always attended normal secular schools, colleges and universities. In America Christian schools, colleges and universities are common. Of course the American pattern shields young people from the harmful influences of a secular or even anti-Christian environment. They may grow up with clean and wholesome attitudes which are uncontaminated by non-Christian culture. British parents may feel somewhat jealous of this. But on the other hand such young people will find it hard to relate to the non-Christian world around them. Life in a holy ghetto does not equip us for effective personal evangelism. Christian educational establishments also rob secular schools of the salt and light which Christian students should contribute.

Because of their particular history many American Christians have developed some rather rigid doctrinal distinctives. Few British Christians know whether their view of Christ's second coming is premillennial, post-millennial or amillennial. This debate hardly touches our churches. But in the United States a sound evangelical faith often goes hand in hand with a premillennial position. As a result premillennialism has frequently been considered a central tenet of the faith. Likewise many will consider that membership of a church which belongs to the World Council of Churches in Geneva disqualifies you as a true believer. This can cause problems overseas in mission. For example the leading Bible schools and seminaries in some countries were founded by such American missionaries, have adopted a premillennial and anti-ecumenical stance and so will not welcome any teachers who hold a different position. This may mean that Europeans will not be able to join their staffs even if they are in other ways well qualified for the job.

For many years American evangelicals were largely opposed to the charismatic renewal. Today this is just beginning to change in some circles. John Wimber's Vineyard churches and some other independent charismatic churches have flourished and grown. They have just begun to have a wider influence but still it remains true that the charismatic renewal dances only at the edges of mainstream evangelical life.

Overseas mission

Statistics on mission are notoriously unreliable, but it is sometimes claimed that some seventy per cent of all missionaries come from the United States. Certainly the strength of Christianity in North America gives birth to a confident and dynamic vision for mission worldwide. As we have already noted, American missionaries do not have a good reputation for cultural sensitivity, language learning or willingness to work under existing Christian leadership locally, but their drive and initiative compensate for this. European missionaries often concentrate on development ministries and on pastoral, Bible teaching work within national churches. It is true that the Third World desperately needs medical, agricultural and other developmental assistance. Likewise overseas churches may excel in other areas of their life, but they are frequently rather weak in quality Bible teaching. While the Europeans edify the church and assist society in these ways, the Americans have more of a vision for evangelism and church planting. Of course these are over-simplified generalisations with many notable exceptions, but one cannot but notice around the world the number of new churches and even denominations which have come into being through American missions. They may be accused of separatism and divisiveness, but through them men and women are finding new life and salvation in Christ.

As a lecturer in mission it impresses me how many of the new ideas about mission stem from American sources. While I dislike much of the jargon which accompanies such new thinking, I have to admit that it seems to capture people's attention and it becomes central to current communication on mission. It is also American mission thinkers who are often in the forefront of rethinking evangelistic strategy as we face the challenging task of mission today. For example, it has been Americans who have led the way concerning 'homogeneous units' in which 'messianic synagogues' and 'messianic mosques' may gather together people of a particular background into churches which are specially suited to their backgrounds. Objections are raised concerning exclusivism, but clearly there is a need for all of us to hear the gospel communicated with our language and cultural forms. We all need Bible teaching which relates to the questions and problems of our background. Worship is more likely to engage our hearts and minds if it uses forms with which we feel comfortable. It is obviously helpful if non-Christians of each race and cultural grouping can see that Christianity relates to them. Thus many people assume that you cannot be a Jew and a Christian at the same time. The existence of specifically Jewish churches gives the lie to such objections. Jewish Christians may therefore be very grateful to our American friends who have pioneered thinking and practice in this as also in so many other areas.

American mission thinkers have not only led the way in mission theory and practice, but also in communication. They have a brilliant way of simplifying complex ideas and expressing them in neat packages with clear diagrams and a host of supporting statistics. However, the resulting over-simplification does not really describe the depths and complexities of people, religions or situations. Often the statistics may be untrue, more the result of guesswork than accuracy. For example, we have no possible means of knowing how many Christians there are in China—estimates range from the unlikely low figure of four million to a fancifully optimistic hundred million. But the statistics of this one huge nation inevitably affect the overall statistics for the world. Recently the ludicrous statistic has been quoted and requoted that in AD 100 there were twelve unreached people groups per congregation of believers! The definition of a 'people group' is far from clear and so we really do not know how many unreached people groups existed in those days. And we have absolutely no possible means of knowing how many Christian congregations there were in AD 100. The statistic does not merit any serious examination, but such clear-cut simple communication grabs the attention, makes a definite impression and influences Christian thinking around the world.

The postman recently delivered a circular from an American organisation informing us of the Christian conferences and consultations we would do well to attend in the coming year if we wanted to keep abreast of mission today. About forty of these were considered of fundamental importance. As they were located in various cities all over the world, you would have to travel widely. Are some people becoming professional conference-goers? The proliferation of such conferences and consultations has gained epidemic proportions. Nevertheless it is good in moderation. Christian workers find it helpful to meet one another to learn from each other and form links of co-operation. Professional consultations on mission among Muslims or other such pressing issues can prove most rewarding. Major conferences like the international Lausanne get-togethers form a stimulus to worldwide mission. And when one attends consultations or conferences of this nature, it is quickly evident that it is Americans who have the finances and organisational skills to run them. This can lead to an unfortunate American domination of international meetings, but without their leadership the whole exercise would probably flounder.

The American missionary movement has developed considerably the potential of short-term workers and of so-called 'tent-makers'. In contemporary western culture young people find it hard to commit themselves long-term to a particular ministry. We live in an age of rapid and frequent change. Few people today remain in one job for more than a few years. So too in mission, candidates think in terms of four or five years, although their knowledge of the local language and culture will inevitably never attain a satisfactory level. They will also not succeed in forming deep personal relationships in cultures where friendships develop slowly. On the other hand short-term workers can fill the many gaps in mission work. They will also learn something from their experience of the church overseas which they can bring back to enrich their home churches.

'Tent-makers' go overseas in their professions, but with the aim also of sharing their Christian faith with local people and playing what part they can in the life of a local church. Such workers will meet with many local people whom the full-time missionary may not be able to reach. They may also be able to help in the church if English is spoken locally. Otherwise they will be isolated through lack of time to learn the language. In some countries 'tent-makers' are purposely trying to stay for a good number of years in order to get right into local society and make deeper personal relationships. Some take the time to learn the local language before going to the country. This is particularly true of those who go to areas of the world which do not allow Christian workers, for example the Muslim world. It is exciting these days to observe the large number of such 'tent-makers' from America and elsewhere in 'closed' countries.

As Europeans we are often suspicious of anything which comes from America and yet we often follow in their footsteps. The influence of the huge Christian church in North America cannot be overestimated. With the immense size and diversity of the American Christian movement there are inevitably weaknesses and failures, but we Europeans need rather to note the great strengths from which we have so much to learn.

8

A FAST-CHANGING WORLD
God's work in Western Europe

Large question marks hang over the future of western Europe. What political and economic implications does 1992 have as the countries of the continent draw more closely into union? What will this mean for the particular countries and regions? In drawing closer together to each other will the European nations isolate themselves from the United States, the British Commonwealth and the rest of the world? As the Soviet Union declines as a super-power, will a federated Europe rival Japan and America economically? And how will future developments affect education, culture and religion?

Computers increasingly determine the course of life today. Those of us who remain computer-illiterate seem quaintly traditional in the fast-moving contemporary world. Pen-pushing clerks have vanished from our banks and offices, computerised telephones have ousted human operators, our supermarket purchases brush past the eagle eye of the computer at the checkout point. Gone are the old days of more intimate personal encounters. Only the few remaining village stores still know their customers personally, call you by name and pause to chat. One day I dared to address the checkout girl at a supermarket and commented on how busy she was that day. She replied with amazement, 'Thank you. You are the first person to talk to me this morning.' The affluence of our fast-moving modern society can easily rob us of our personal relationships. Western society is suffering from this depersonalisation. And many people feel they no longer have meaning or value.

Rapid and constant change characterise modern life. No longer do we remain faithful to one particular brand of petrol for our car; a small incentive sends us rushing to open an account with a different bank or building society; mid-career changes of profession give renewed job satisfaction. Change prevents boredom, the great enemy of today's western world. We see these cultural developments affecting Christians too. Many feel free to move from church to church to satisfy their own tastes in worship, teaching or styles of leadership.

Marriage too comes under threat not only through this desire for change, but also from the pressures of work. The ambition to succeed and to get money drives people to work long hours and so have little free time with their marriage partner and children. At home the television drowns out all meaningful communication and marriages drift apart. The lack of real happiness at home then pushes people to stay longer at work, spend the evenings in the pub or escape through some sporting hobby. Thus a vicious circle develops which frequently leads to divorce and misery. A few years ago I did a small survey among men who were fishing in our local river. Over ninety per cent declared that they came fishing in order to gain 'a bit of peace from the wife and kids'.

Sadly these social problems in Europe undermine the life of the church too. We know from the New Testament that the sins of the world easily infiltrate the church, so we are not surprised. But it presents us with a challenge. European churches are becoming more aware of their need to give their people the real sense of community which our society lacks. Fellowship and relationships have become vitally important. Faced with the insecurities of modern life and its consequent personal heartaches, Christians in Europe today strongly emphasise pastoral counselling, marriage enrichment and the care of the elderly. Theological colleges and Bible schools now train students pastorally, realising that preparation for Christian ministry does not just mean filling students' heads with theology. The danger in Europe at present may be that we are swinging the pendulum too far. Theology and biblical study have sometimes been edged out of church life in favour of pastoral sensitivity and subjective spirituality.

Catholic and Protestant

Traditionally western Europe has been divided into two overall groupings, the largely Protestant nations in the north and the Roman Catholic countries in the south. Today this division has begun to diminish. The whole continent is equally afflicted with materialistic secularism and unbelief. The traditional forms of Catholicism and Protestantism have failed to satisfy the mass of our populations, leading to a widespread disaffection with the church. A spiritual hunger remains. Dynamic and culturally relevant churches still attract good congregations. Yet many people today seek spiritual reality and satisfaction through eastern mysticism or the occult.

The Roman Catholic church

Protestants sometimes think of the Catholic church as a monolithic unity, but actually a variety of currents flow through the church and produce different movements. For simplicity's sake we may define four main movements within contemporary Catholicism.

1. *The traditional*

The present Pope, supported by the Curia in the Vatican, strongly upholds the traditions of Catholic theology, spirituality and ethics. This section of the church does not change in its beliefs about the infallibility of the Pope, the role of Mary and the saints, the old sacramental doctrines, celibacy of the priesthood, and opposition to all birth control. When the Pope visits anywhere he always makes a point of praying at the main local shrine to Mary. Protestants have to realise the strength of such folk religion in traditional Catholic communities.

2. *Liberal and political*

In reaction against traditionalism, and often influenced by Protestant thought, some today embrace radical liberal theology and biblical criticism. Sadly such people fail to see the consequences of such destructive approaches in the history of the Protestant churches, where the spread of liberalism and the undermining of faith in the reliability of the Bible gradually emptied our churches.

Many within the Catholic church have also reacted against the power of a hierarchical church which inevitably aligned itself with state authorities and the rich. Latin American liberation theology too has swept through the church. Social and political involvement in support of the oppressed and the poor has become an integral part of contemporary Catholic thought. While most of us would rejoice in this development, we have also to note the danger that liberation of the oppressed can replace rather than supplement the work of Christ in his death for our sin. Salvation from oppression in this world can become more important than eternal life and reconciliation with God himself.

3. Biblical renewal

In Reformation days Catholic bonfires destroyed Bibles and their translators. How things have changed! Today Catholics are strongly encouraged to read their Bibles and the church plays an active part in distributing the Scriptures. Inevitably the reading of the Bible can influence people's beliefs. For example, one priest has openly declared that he will no longer preach about purgatory, for he does not find this teaching in the Bible. Through Bible reading the centrality of Jesus Christ is becoming a new reality for some.

4. Charismatic renewal

A sophisticated young teacher told me enthusiastically how she had been filled with the Spirit and so had a new warmth of love and faith. Eventually it became clear however that Jesus remained quite secondary to her, for her spiritual experience had merely reinforced her love for the Virgin Mary. In contrast to this the Vicar General of a Scandinavian Catholic church told me how his charismatic experience had made Jesus and the Bible central to his whole faith. Sometimes the charismatic renewal merely warms and enlivens traditional Catholic religion; in other cases the Holy Spirit is doing his work of glorifying Christ in our lives and opening the Scriptures to us.

Protestant churches

For simplicity's sake we may divide Protestantism into three categories—state or mainline churches, free churches and newer charismatic churches. Increasingly these three groupings relate and work together more closely in opposition to the inroads of secular atheism, eastern religions, New Age and the occult.

1. Mainline churches

Throughout western Europe these Reformation churches face twin dangers: liberalism, which undermines the very foundations of the Christian faith, and traditionalism, which stifles vitality in the dreary cottonwool of irrelevance. In the struggle against liberal innovations it is easy to resist all attempts to make the life and worship of the church contemporary. In pastoral love and graciousness we may submit to the wishes of older members who dislike change, and in so doing alienate the unchurched and the younger generation. Boredom is the one thing young people today will not tolerate.

Happily we are witnessing today new movements of life in these mainline churches. A new freedom and a spirit of adventure have transformed many congregations, so many churches are growing again after years of decline. In Norway evangelical theology defeated the liberals in the last century, and the Lutheran state church remained spiritually strong until secularism opened the door to liberalism. But now revival movements are again renewing the church. In Britain steady decline has characterised the Anglican church for years, but now the downward slope of the graph has begun to turn upwards. The much heralded decade of evangelism in the 1990s sees the Anglican church ready for growth. The appointment of an evangelical as the new archbishop will surely help.

Throughout western Europe it is the mainline churches which hold the key to any possibility of a general turning back to Christ. These churches are in the main bloodstream of national cultures, and they can influence the whole world-view of their peoples. We need to pray much for them.

2. *Free churches*

Strangely the so-called 'free' churches sometimes face a particular danger of cultural stagnation and conservatism. On the other hand they have often remained faithful to Scripture and Christ when the mainline churches surrendered to the onslaughts of liberalism. With their freer organisational structures comes the opportunity to relate flexibly to modern society without compromising their faith in Christ. While the evangelical churches in Germany and Switzerland often fail to change with the times despite their members' warm love for the Lord and his word, in Holland and increasingly in Britain signs of adventurous life are emerging. Sadly in southern Europe the ghetto mentality of evangelicals in formerly strongly Catholic or Greek Orthodox societies still prevents the churches from effective witness in increasingly secular surroundings.

3. Newer charismatic churches

The growth point of the church in Europe in recent years has been the charismatic renewal and the new churches which have emerged as a result of it. That is not to say that growth has not taken place elsewhere, for we have already observed for example that evangelical Anglican churches have also flourished. Yet it is principally the charismatic renewal which has introduced a new life and vitality into many traditional churches. New songs have multiplied with the renewed emphasis on worship. Many Christians have found liberty and a freshness of faith as they have come into the experience of spiritual gifts.

The advent of the charismatic movement has unfortunately brought some traumas as well as rich blessing. It has often divided churches, so that disunity and bitterness have pushed love to one side. Happily we see a growing desire now to quash that spirit of rivalry and replace it with harmonious co-operation. Perhaps the decade of evangelism will further cement this growing desire to work together.

The charismatic emphasis on direct prophetic words from God has sometimes led to an unfortunate weakness in theology and careful biblical exegesis, but this is not always the case and some are coming back to sound biblical teaching and preaching. Likewise the early over-emphasis on miraculous healing has given way more and more to an awareness that in God's grace suffering of all sorts may not always be clearly demonic. More recently spiritual warfare has come into prominence and we still often lack a careful biblical approach on this subject. But in many parts of the world, not only in Europe, the charismatic movement has really helped the church to face the realities of Satan, demonic activity and the occult.

The largest Bible School in Europe is in Uppsala, Sweden. The Word of Life Bible School attracts hundreds of young people with its dynamic and youthful enthusiasm. Sadly its teaching strongly emphasises that God blesses people of faith with material prosperity. They stress that all sickness comes from Satan and Christians ought not to suffer. They deduce that Job suffered as he did because of his own lack of trust in the Lord. Prosperity teaching of this sort works like a magnet, drawing young people to a triumphalistic confidence in their faith. It fits the materialism of western Europe as well as the whites of South Africa, among whom this teaching is also strong. Sadly it gains ground too in eastern Europe where many people covet the wealth of the capitalistic west. It is easy for them to equate atheism with poverty and Christian faith with material wealth.

Issues in the church

1. Pluralism

Christians today face the fact of other religions on their doorsteps. Muslims, Sikhs, Hindus, Buddhists and Jews have flocked to our cities. In our schools children receive teaching about other faiths and learn to appreciate them. More and more Christians begin to question the uniqueness of Christ and the Christian faith. The question of the Christian approach to other religions burns hotly.[3] This issue has also emerged as the front-runner objection to the gospel among non-Christians— 'What's so special about Jesus? Why Jesus rather than Krishna or Mohammed?'

The focus of this issue has sometimes centred on the question of whether Jews should be evangelised. As we have seen, some Christians feel that Jews have their own way to God through the Old Testament covenants, while Jesus came to open the door for Gentiles. They maintain then that Jews do not need the gospel of Jesus Christ. They also affirm that in the light of the church's history of persecution of Jews, Christians have no right to share their faith with Jews. It is then pointed out that if Jews can find salvation without Jesus, so can monotheistic Muslims and indeed people of other religions also. In fact, all evangelism becomes an unwanted arrogance.

Biblical Christians need to address these questions seriously.

2. Oppression

No longer are European Christians merely interested in personal salvation and our spiritual relationship with God. The claims of the oppressed have touched our hearts and entered our theological thinking. We have begun to see God's concern for the widow, the orphan, the poor and the oppressed. This applies to those who suffer socio-political injustice, and also to the victims of racial discrimination. While Christians are themselves not innocent of racial prejudice, we stand with our black friends in South Africa as well as in our own continent.

As Christians we have just begun to be aware too of the question of sexism. No longer can we get away with sexist language, using 'man' for humanity etc. The role of women in society and in the church has become a hot potato. But we have hardly yet come to grips with the question of 'speciesism'—the human domination over and misuse of non-human species and of our environment.

3. Moral issues

With the decline of Christianity in most West European societies, immorality has become more obvious around us. The sins of the world have a way of influencing the church too. Debate rages therefore on abortion, homosexuality, pre-marital sex, divorce, excessive use of alcohol and drugs. The younger generation in the church cries out for help and teaching on these topics, but often older Christians have become either unthinkingly legalistic or unbiblically permissive. Sometimes these issues go hand in hand with occult practices which have become so common in our societies today.

Evangelism

In the 1960s the churches faced their steady decline by dreaming nostalgically of revival returning to our countries as it had in previous centuries. In the 1970s we saw the need to revitalise the life of the church as a prerequisite for any future evangelism. In the 1980s more churches began to move out in evangelism, but often their forms of worship and church life militated against effective outreach. Over the centuries we have fitted our structures around feeding fish in our church aquariums rather than becoming 'fishers of men'.

Now in this decade of evangelism we face the challenge of bringing our countries back to the gospel of Christ. It is encouraging to note some media interest in Christian things—are we becoming more newsworthy? Realising the immense influence of the media it is vital that biblical Christians gain a hearing not only in the newspapers, magazines and local as well as national radio, but also and particularly on television.

In our renewed concern for evangelism and church planting in Europe we are confronted with the danger of insularity. We may become so caught up in our passion for winning our own countries that we lose our missionary vision for the rest of the world. Jesus himself taught that it is actually more blessed to give than just to receive. This truth relates well to our situation. If we fail to give sacrificially to other areas of mission, we shall experience how God will not bless us in our home mission. The churches overseas may lack many things in which we may be able to minister to them, but they do have considerable experience in evangelism. Many Christians overseas have assumed that church planting is a normal part of the Christian life. They have much to contribute to us in this decade. In giving to them we shall ourselves receive.

Conclusion

Western Europe has experienced long years of spiritual decline which has emptied our churches. Today few merely traditional church-goers remain. The church has generally become slimmer but fitter. Together with an increasing dynamic within the church itself we may also observe among some non-Christians a growing disillusionment with materialism and the rat-race. While some look for answers in the dark world of the occult and even witchcraft, others seek solace in eastern religions and New Age. But an open door presents itself also to churches which have confidence in their message of Christ and witness to the gospel with cultural relevance and obvious spirituality.

As this decade of evangelism progresses it seems that the church in Britain and parts of Scandinavia may be well placed to take advantage of the open doors God has given us. Holland too has many churches which are in a good position to grow. In some other countries a narrow conservatism and even a ghetto mentality may sadly stifle effective outreach and hinder the possibilities of church growth.

May God's word and Holy Spirit impart true life to us all in our various churches and send us out in effective evangelism in this decade.

9

THE DEATH OF MARXISM IN THE YEAR OF REVOLUTIONS

God at work in Eastern Europe

Future students will all learn about 1989 as a turning point in world history. While 1917 saw the beginning of the Marxist experiment, 1989 witnessed the final collapse of a dead system. Many of us watched our TV screens and saw the immense crowds thronging the cities of eastern Europe and toppling the apparently impregnable might of Communist regimes. The outward appearance of power hid the rotten core of economic, spiritual, social and moral breakdown. Eastern Europe has set out on a new path which will not be an easy one. Europe's years of iron-curtained division have come to an end.

Through television we have learned of the fearful economic chaos which Marxism has brought to the countries of eastern Europe. Thus Russians joke about the nationality of Adam and Eve. Were they English, French or ...? No, they were certainly Russian. Only Russians could share one apple between two people, have nothing but fig leaves for clothes and still call it paradise. We have seen pictures of empty shelves in the shops. But did our television convey adequately the vital role played by the churches in these revolutions? In almost every situation the church formed the foundation for the new movements of freedom, peace and truth.

When visiting Czechoslovakia after the revolution I was told of the importance of truth. They joked that the main Russian newspaper *Pravda*, (which means 'Truth') contains no truth, while the other newspaper *Izvestia* ('News') has no news. They claimed that only the church could be trusted to speak truth. They also talked of the mass demonstrations in Wenceslas Square and the damp November evening when two secret policemen were discovered on the edge of the crowd. Would they be lynched, their limbs torn from their bodies in mass hatred and revenge? Just at that moment a church minister climbed the platform and called on the crowds to kneel and pray the Lord's Prayer—'Forgive us our trespasses as we forgive them that trespass against us'. Many told me how that moment turned their revolution from bitter revenge to forgiving love and kindness. These lovely Christian characteristics have formed the foundation of the revolution and the new society which must now be developed. What will they build on that foundation?

This is the challenge to the Christian church. Communism has left a spiritual vacuum as its legacy. Will the Christian church fill the emptiness with the practical and spiritual truth of Jesus Christ, or will western materialism draw the multitudes of eastern Europe to dedicate their lives to

Mammon? After years of drab poverty the glitter of western capitalism and the consumer society beckons almost irresistibly. From the fringes of Christianity extreme 'prosperity' teaching draws people with its simplistic promises that faith in Christ will always bring material blessings and will save from suffering and sickness. The vacuum is also being filled by eastern religious sects and New Age movements. Yoga and Zen meditation have flooded into these countries.

What then of the church? Western Christians dare not criticise our brothers and sisters who have suffered for Christ, endured long decades of fierce persecution and anti-religious propaganda, but have won through. Who would have thought twenty years ago that the mighty power of communism would crumble so quickly and that the poor, oppressed churches would triumph? We cannot but praise God for his faithfulness and grace. Now we need to pray for the churches as they face the new challenges in situations of freedom. In many ways they are ill prepared for this and, humanly speaking, they could easily lose the battle of the future.

For many years in most east European situations it has been impossible to invite non-Christians to church services. Evangelism took place on a one-to-one basis. Then after commitment to Christ new Christians would dare to join their brothers and sisters in more public worship. This has meant that church services were aimed at definitely committed Christians who were willing to pay the price of active persecution. Going to church often meant losing one's job, even being sent to prison. One Russian church elder told me that most of his members had spent time in prison for their faith. Worship therefore was serious, not intended at all to entertain. The danger for the future is that we may lose the younger generation and also fail to attract into the church those who at present are looking for an ideology by which to live. Western churches have much to learn about serious faith, absolute commitment to Christ and a willingness to suffer for him. But perhaps we may also have something to contribute in our more joyful and lively forms of worship.

The church needs to fill the ideological vacuum, but then also to demonstrate how Christian faith gives a love and joy which satisfies every aspect of our personalities. This came home to me when I was in Prague after the 1989 revolution. A middle-aged man came to the church where I was speaking and informed me that he had never before visited a church. He then told me that until recently he had been professor of atheism in the prestigious local university, but was now out of a job as atheism had become unacceptable. He was asking about Christianity—can an intelligent professor believe in Christianity? What does it mean for practical living if one becomes a Christian? What is involved in joining the church? Happily that particular church was well suited to meeting his needs and he enjoyed its style of teaching and worship. But will that be equally true for the up-and-coming generation?

The East European situation compels us to look again at the Bible, our message and how we present it.

1. *The biblical message*

The unchanging message of God's coming to the world in the person of Jesus Christ, his death for our sins, his resurrection to bring us new life and his final second coming in glory—all that remains the same whether it is preached in eastern Europe or anywhere else. But it may have important different applications and emphases. For example, after years of persecution and pressure some church leaders as well as many ordinary Christians have compromised with the Marxist state authorities. For them the cross of Christ signifies an open door to forgiveness. For others who have suffered for their faith the cross demonstrates a God who knows what it means to suffer, and the resurrection may show that the sometimes traumatic after-effects of long years of persecution can yield in Christ to a new life of joyful victory.

In recent visits to the Soviet Union and eastern Europe I have been impressed by the vital relevance of Paul's cosmic understanding of God's saving work in Christ. In Colossians 1:15–20 the repeated emphasis on 'all' underlines the reality that Christ's redeeming purposes extend not only to all peoples everywhere, but also to the whole creation. In the ecological disaster of eastern Europe it is highly relevant to point out that in the Bible we are intimately linked to our environment. Human sin brings tragedy to nature, godly obedience to the Lord leads to harmony in nature. Christians in eastern Europe can look forward to the climax of history when God will not only redeem us and there will be a new humanity, but he will also redeem all things and creation will be renewed. No longer will sin corrupt us and our societies, nor will pollution poison the earth—even the desert that was the Aral Sea will have new life in Christ. What a message of good news! Unfortunately it still seems a distant dream.

In this post-Marxist age Jesus Christ and his church bring good news. In a society where no one trusted anyone else, the biblical emphasis on loving relationships brings a smile to dead-pan faces. Christ's humility as the servant can renew society as people begin again to learn the values of courtesy, gracious humility and service of others. In our churches in the west unfortunately little emphasis is given to biblical teaching on truth, but after years of Marxist propaganda and fear the central importance of truth takes on new meaning. Christians have much to contribute as they live and speak truth. All these great realities of the gospel of Christ can flow freely when Jesus Christ becomes the centre of our lives both as individuals and in society. In the spiritual vacuum which results from the death of Marxist atheism we have to ask again whether the church is prepared to live and preach such a relevant gospel. If it does not, will Marxist dialectical materialism be replaced by western secular materialism plus a spiritual drug-injection of eastern religious mysticism or the western-style blandishment of crass 'prosperity' teaching?

2. Communication

For several decades it has been extremely dangerous to evangelise openly in eastern Europe, but more recently Christians have been attempting to reach out publicly. In Moscow airport I heard a group of Pentecostals singing and preaching in the entrance hall. While admiring their zeal and courage I also sensed that their patterns of communication failed to attract people. In Central Asia too Christians now preach and witness in the parks, but one wonders how far their methods are attuned to their non-Christian hearers. As yet, such public witness is relatively new, so hopefully Christians will quickly learn to adopt new approaches which will appeal to non-Christians. Perhaps some western Christians may be able with humble sensitivity to suggest the use of drama, more contemporary music or even symbolic dance. If these are introduced too quickly or without cultural sensitivity, Christians will not be able to accept them. But gently and gradually we may be able to encourage local Christians to experiment in forms which are culturally suited.

A group of young Czech Christian leaders were discussing how best to work in the new situation of religious freedom. One suggested that we need more Christian literature to teach and train Christians in biblical truth and mission. Then they talked about literature which could be used in evangelism to answer the questions which are commonly asked by people with an atheistic Marxist background. One young man objected, claiming that under communism anything written was a lie, so people would assume that Christian literature too was propagandist untruth. Much debate ensued, but finally all agreed that we need more literature but that it must be so written that readers would clearly see that it is not just propaganda.

Later I saw a lay-training course produced by Christians in the west. It started with the question 'Who is Jesus?' and then gave the short, simple answer 'Jesus is God' with three biblical verses to prove it. The style resembled communist propaganda and made it unusable in eastern Europe without considerable change.

It remains true however that eastern Europe desperately needs a wider range of Christian literature. There are so few commentaries to help pastors and other Christians to study and teach the Bible. They lack basic books on Christian doctrine and teaching to help people appreciate the riches of the faith and be able to discern between true and unbalanced emphases. Devotional books, books on practical Christian living, books for children and young people, Sunday school teaching aids, help for Christians to understand Islam and eastern religions in such a way that they can witness effectively—so much is needed. In the west we have such a wealth of Christian literature of all sorts; eastern Europe lacks this.

Traditional churches

As Protestants in western Europe our attention goes all too easily to parallel churches in the east to the exclusion of more traditional churches. It remains true however that the majority of Christians still belong to these old mainline denominations. The Roman Catholic and Orthodox churches claim the allegiance of millions, as does the Lutheran church in the eastern part of Germany. In the 1989 revolutions Christians from these churches often led the freedom movements and the early demonstrations and rallies found their focus in a church building belonging to them. We observed this particularly in the Solidarity movement with its close ties to the Roman Catholic church.

Frequently these churches represent local populations in new forms of nationalism. The

Polish Roman Catholic church is the focal point for a national messianism in opposition to Russian domination. Equally in the Baltic states the traditional Lutheran and Catholic churches have become the focus for national identity. In the Ukraine and various other Soviet republics independence movements are closely linked to the national church. These denominations are deeply bedded in the whole culture of their people.

It was a moving experience to attend a Saturday early morning service in an Orthodox church in Soviet Central Asia. About a thousand people stood for three hours in the crowded church as the solemn chanting of the liturgy gradually unfolded. Standing next to an old lady I was humbled to think that she was probably born at about the time of the 1917 Communist revolution. All the people around me had been brought up under intense atheistic propaganda and fierce discrimination against Christians. Despite those long years of opposition and persecution they had stood firm and their faith had vanquished the might of Marxism. There were no liturgy books but many of those present joined in the chants, knowing them off by heart. There had been no Sunday schools or religious education for the youth, but still they knew the words of the very lengthy liturgy. I watched a young woman earnestly praying on her own at the back of the church; after a while the tears began to roll down her cheeks as she poured out her prayers. As an evangelical Christian I may have some doubts about the theology of these churches and I may long for a biblical renewal which would reduce the importance given to Mary, the saints and the ikons. On the other hand I cannot but be impressed by the spirituality of these churches and by the fact that they are so firmly rooted in their local cultures. We dare not ignore their significance for the future witness of the Christian faith in this part of the world. Young people flow into these churches to join the elderly and often uneducated Christians who have survived the furnace of Communist persecution.

Nevertheless the cutting edge of biblical evangelism remains in more evangelical circles. Baptists, Pentecostals and other evangelical denominations have grown considerably since the 1989 revolutions. As we have already observed, they are often rather serious and outwardly rather old-fashioned and legalistic, but through the years they have maintained a strongly Christ-centred faith and good biblical teaching.

In these days they gain much from the many western Christians who come in with teaching and literature—one church in Romania has had foreign visitors preaching every Sunday for a year—but the advantages of this fellowship include also real dangers. With the present freedom these churches are flooded with foreign visitors, all of whom bring financial gifts plus their own brands of Christian teaching—different attitudes to the charismatic renewal, various taboos of legalism, every shade of theology about the millennium, baptism and church order. Chaos and divisions easily ensue. Churches sometimes begin to waste their energies on internal wrangles imported from the west rather than concentrating their united efforts on the great open doors for evangelism today. How one wishes that Christians from the west would demonstrate more humility and wisdom in their approaches to mission in eastern Europe! We need to be much more sensitive and submit to the wishes of national church leaders.

Conclusion

Gorbachev and his 'perestroika' have unleashed all sorts of new forces in eastern Europe. How will things evolve in the coming years? All eyes are directed towards Germany to see how this united people will develop. How will they manage the radically different economic situations of the two parts of Germany? Will the people of what was East Germany be colonised by the prosperous and powerful west? The long-term answer to such questions may determine the extent of any future opening of borders between the two halves of Europe.

And what will happen to the Soviet Union itself? Nationalisms and a disastrous economic collapse threaten violent unrest and disaster. Atheism with its concern for classes rather than individuals has stifled the life of the whole culture—it is a rare treat to see anyone smiling in public. The cultural, economic and political developments will of course radically affect the church, its life and growth. In Muslim Central Asia, with its population of some sixty million people, the threat to the church looms like a heavy grey cloud. If that area separated from the Soviet Union and became an independent Muslim state, then the church could well face a new wave of oppression. Because the church largely consists of Russians, rather than central Asian peoples, the persecution would be tied in with nationalistic racialism. Christians are already aware of the dangers.

And what about the future for the other former communist countries? Inevitably they watch the experiment in the united Germany and the chaotic uncertainty of the Soviet Union with considerable interest.

In western Europe we should ask the question, 'Will eastern Europe influence us or can it only be the reverse?' Will our capitalistic materialism bring them all the wealth which we enjoy, but also all our social and moral problems? Is it possible that their situation would influence our way of thinking? In eastern Europe atheism has been totally discredited and has become untenable as a philosophy, while religion is seen to have truth. Western Europe has much to learn from the tragic experiences of eastern Europe under Marxist atheism.

10

HOW ON EARTH DOES GOD WORK?

In this small book we have done a whistle-stop trip around the world to see something of what God is doing in different areas. Inevitably our jet has overflown some parts of the world where different readers would have preferred to stop and visit. Having lived in Bermuda for some years in my youth I am very aware that no mention has been made of the Caribbean islands or the other small islands in the Atlantic Ocean. Likewise we have not discussed the multitudes of island states in the south Pacific. And within the continents and groups which we have noted there are doubtless many significant omissions. In one small book we cannot examine every race and people.

As author, one can only plead guilty to these failures. In defence it has to be said that the aim of this book was not to give detailed information concerning every aspect of God's work in every part of the world. The closest approximation to such a mammoth work is the *World Christian Encyclopedia* by David Barrett.[4]

Nevertheless we have sketched out the widespread

growth of God's church in the various continents. As Christians we rejoice in the fact that we have the privilege in Christ of belonging to this huge family all around the world in every country. In our days we have opportunities for travel which our grandparents could hardly envisage. This allows us to experience the reality of loving relationships with sisters and brothers of different races and backgrounds.

The rate of change is startling. If we look back a hundred years the churches in most parts of Asia and Sub-Saharan Africa were either non-existent or still in their infancy. The Protestant movement in Latin America had hardly begun, while the traditional mixture of animistic tribal religion with a veneer of Roman Catholicism dominated people's allegiance. Even in the great international mission conference in Edinburgh in 1910 there were no indigenous delegates from the Third World. This demonstrates the radically progressive character of such pioneer missionaries as Hudson Taylor in China who was already emphasising the vital importance of indigenous Christian leadership in the second half of the nineteenth century. Henry Venn and other great Anglican leaders in the nineteenth century had the same vision for the churches in Africa.

In the 1960s many critics predicted that the end of colonialism would lead inevitably to the death of the Christian churches in previously colonial areas. Prediction can be a dangerous game! Political independence encouraged the churches to develop their own national leadership. Under their own leaders the churches began to multiply and in the last thirty years millions of new Christians have flocked into the churches, particularly in Africa, but also in some countries of Asia. In Latin America a more tolerant and open-hearted attitude by the Roman Catholic church since the second Vatican Council has opened the door for the work of the Holy Spirit in the mushrooming growth of Pentecostal, Baptist and other Protestant churches.

The 1974 Lausanne Conference formed a watershed for the development of evangelical churches. Until then few Third World Christian leaders were well known outside their own countries. But at Lausanne new household names emerged, particularly from Latin America and Africa. From Lausanne too there developed an urgent call for theological and biblical training in every part of the world. As a result many new Bible schools and theological colleges came into being with ever-increasing standards both academically and practically. Today we salute the widespread achievements of these training establishments. Large numbers of men and women of high spiritual and academic calibre have been well trained for leadership in local churches and in wider mission. No longer can western Christians look down their paternalistic noses as they relate to their brothers and sisters in other parts of the world. In fact today the boot may have slipped onto the other foot, for generally it is not the western churches which manifest vitality and growth. It is often within the Third World churches that the tension between academic theological training and practical spiritual dynamic is being resolved. Sadly in the western churches those who are sound in biblical and theological study sometimes stand apart from the vision of dynamic out-going evangelism and mission. Likewise, those who experience the vitality of the Holy Spirit both in their personal lives and in their mission sometimes show scant regard for a careful and disciplined study of the Bible and theology. The west has much to learn from others in these days. But we rejoice in the working of God in his church around the world.

As we have noted, 1989 marked the end of the rule of Communism in so many lands. It has been remarkable since then to observe the victory of the often poor and uneducated church over the apparently powerful forces of atheism. Despite years of propaganda and persecution which marginalised the church, God's people have held on to their faith. In the Soviet Union church membership nosedived in the first ten years or so of Communist opposition, but since then the church has been able to hold steady and then in more recent years to show remarkable growth. Statistics are unreliable, but some people estimate that at least ten per cent of the entire population attends church on a Sunday. Most of these are of course in the Russian Orthodox church, although the Baptists and Pentecostals also have significant congregations.

In China under Chairman Mao Christians had to go underground to a large extent. Many in the west thought that Chinese Christianity had met its end. But God remained on the throne of China and he has kept his people wonderfully. At the time of the Marxist revolution the church in China was relatively small with only a million or two members. Leadership often still lay in missionary hands, so that the church sometimes appeared to be just a copy of western models. Through the fires of fierce persecution and fearful suffering the church has not only been purified, but millions of new Christians have been added to the church. Of course such horrific persecution always leaves intense problems in its wake and western observers should not be naive about the life of the church in formerly communist countries. Lack of teaching, stubborn traditionalism, disunity and mutual suspicion or lack of trust all remain as a legacy from the rule of communism. It would be wrong to idealise the church in China, but with deeply thankful hearts we recognise the work of the Holy Spirit in giving his people an almost incredible endurance against terrible odds.

While western Christians love to enthuse about the life and growth of churches overseas, it has become fashionable to contrast this with stagnation and lifelessness in Europe. The demise of colonialism led at first to a bullish optimism in newly independent countries, but in Europe it has introduced a deeply self-critical sense of inferiority. Liberal criticism and secular materialism have combined to empty those churches which have not kept up to date in their presentation of an assured Christian message. Large numbers of traditional church-goers have left the churches. The increasing pressures of hectic busy lives have pushed people away from involvement in the church. As a result church statistics have drifted downwards for several decades, but towards the end of the 1980s this trend has been reversed. Religion and spirituality are back on the world's agenda.

Particularly the newer charismatic 'House Churches' and the more charismatic churches within the denominations have grown in numbers and influence. Their dynamic, exuberant disco-style worship and optimistic confidence give a cutting edge to their faith in a God who is alive today. Other evangelicals may note the often rather careless use of Scripture, but people are attracted to more youthful Christian forms and their emphasis on a God who not only works miracles but also speaks in prophecy directly to his people. Now they underline the spiritual battle against demonic powers. Of course there is a danger in every over-emphasised fad or fashion, but this emphasis on spiritual warfare relates closely to the growth of occultism through a revival of paganism, the spread of eastern religions together with New Age movements and a multitude of other spirit-related practices like astrology, ouija boards or the Dungeons and Dragons game.

Although the charismatic churches make considerable gains these days, we need a balanced analysis which takes note of the fact that they are by no means alone in seeing success. In the cities we shall find large non-charismatic churches which also flourish and grow. And in village after village struggling little churches with tiny handfuls of church-goers have come to life during this past decade and have grown. Perhaps they only had ten or fifteen in their services ten years ago and now have increased to fifty. Such little churches will not hit the headlines, nor will they trumpet their successes in the media, but we are living through days of spiritual upturn. In my own village, for example, the local Anglican church struggled with a mere fifteen on a Sunday just a few years ago; now we enjoy a warm fellowship with about seventy or eighty adults on a Sunday. Most of the village churches in our area have experienced growth in the last few years with a change to more biblical and evangelical ministries. The Lord is at work in Europe too!

Bible translation

Since the Second World War God has given Christians a determined desire to get the Bible translated into all the many languages in every part of the world. The professional expertise of Wycliffe Bible Translators has led the way. They have sent large numbers of their members into many tribal groups to reduce their languages to writing, teach people to read and also translate God's word. Their linguistic expertise has been passed on to missionaries in many other missionary societies so that this vital work may be achieved more effectively and speedily. In some countries national translation societies have been established through the work of Wycliffe Bible Translators so that local people can do the work of translation without being subject to foreign bodies.

In many situations the existing Bible translations in national languages were made a long time ago and have become outdated. My wife and I remember the excitement and hunger when a revised New Testament in our local language in Indonesia came into print. At first we had to ration it, only allowing two copies into each village church until larger stocks became available. As we know from European church history, God's Holy Spirit changes lives and whole societies when the Bible is widely read by people in their own language. We also know how vital it has been in English to have more modern translations which ordinary people can read easily.

Every year we see a flow of Bible translations coming into print. One by one the thousands of different languages have God's word translated into them. On a recent visit to Soviet Central Asia it was exciting to visit someone who was busily translating the New Testament into a major local language. Matthew and Mark were already in print, Luke and John were making progress. The rest of the New Testament still lay in the future. And there are still many other languages which await translations. Well trained workers are needed. But it is exciting to note the tremendous progress which has been made over recent years.

Training

The life and growth of the church under the Holy Spirit depends largely on the development of well trained leaders with spiritual vitality. Training for church leadership stands at the head of any list of mission priorities. We have already observed the spread of Bible schools and theological colleges in the Third World since the 1974 Lausanne Conference. Increasingly evangelicals have begun to take biblical and theological studies much more seriously, so that they can play a major part in giving the lectures and writing the books which form the thinking of the next generation of church leaders—and then through them their ordinary church members.

But generally speaking full-time theological colleges and Bible schools can only train a relatively small number of top leaders. Expanding churches need more than this. Latin America has seen the development of many 'night Bible institutes' in which people study after their day's work. Latin America also pioneered theological education by extension, a system in which the lecturers travel out to groups of students in their home areas rather than students gathering in the centralised Bible school. In this way groups of Christians can meet in their housing area or village each week to discuss the previous week's private study, gain further input from the lecturer and also enjoy the fellowship and interaction of the group. Theological education by extension has widened out from its original Latin American base, being used now in every continent. It has the potential of being able to train Christian leaders at every level in much larger numbers.

More and more churches in Europe and elsewhere have become aware of the vital significance of training Christians biblically and practically for evangelism and service. Some local churches have started one year programmes of teaching and training. Sometimes groups of churches from the same denomination or in the same locality have clubbed together to run such training programmes. Of course these local initiatives may lack the theological or mission expertise of a full-time establishment, but they play a significant role in training Christians for service locally.

It is encouraging to see the adventurous spirit with which Christians are experimenting with new forms of training for Christian leadership and service. This growth of evangelical scholarship in biblical, theological and other related subjects bodes well for the future of God's church.

Social awareness

In the past evangelicals were often accused of being only interested in people's souls with little concern for their bodies. Actually a more careful reading of missionary records shows considerable emphasis on social ministries and even political involvement for the sake of those suffering discrimination. On the other hand, evangelical magazines and other writings have sometimes played down social and political concerns because they knew their constituencies' dislike of a theologically liberal 'social gospel'.

Today evangelical Christians have jumped on the bandwagon of concern for the oppressed. We have become deeply aware of the biblical emphasis on justice and God's love for the poor. Indeed there is sometimes a danger that we can lose sight of our traditional belief in personal sin and in reconciliation with God through the atoning death of Jesus Christ on the cross. But no one today can justifiably accuse evangelical Christians of being unthinking right-wing traditionalists. It is encouraging to notice a passionate concern which has led to pioneering work for drug addicts, AIDS sufferers, the homeless and other suffering or marginalised people. Evangelical Christians play a significant part today in pressure groups working for greater justice. Of course more still could be done and there are still many who lack such concern, but God's Holy Spirit is moving his people to love their needy neighbours.

Sadly the tension between God-centred spiritual ministries and more neighbour-centred social concerns remains. Much thought has gone into mission theories which stress the inseparable nature of these two emphases, but more needs to be done. It is often pointed out that social ministries are not just tin-openers to prepare the way for evangelism, but are in themselves an essential part of Christian mission. Yet those who emphasise this truth sometimes have less sympathy for fellow Christians who concentrate on purely evangelistic mission.

While it is often noted that social ministry does frequently lead to more effective evangelism, few seem to believe that a right relationship with God might bring social and even political benefits. This is understandable, for history presents us with too many cases where committed Christians have failed totally to stand for the rights of the oppressed. Likewise we see too many committed Christians who are deeply involved in loving work for marginalised minorities and even in political action for the sake of justice, but who seem to ignore people's need for evangelism and eternal life. We need therefore to be reminded again and again that evangelism does often lead to social change.

In our area of Indonesia it was not acceptable for men to do any muscular work until people became Christians. Then men began to join their wives in the fields. This not only changed the local economy for the better, but also brought a greater sense of oneness into marriage relationships. In the fertile Kathmandu valley in Nepal the animistic spirits in the local Hindu religion have forbidden people to use any machinery in agriculture or transport in the valley. This seriously hinders agricultural productivity. If the people of Nepal became Christians, it would lead also to more food through better agriculture.

In our day God is at work, moving Christians to rethink the relationship of the gospel to political, social and ecological issues, and then motivating them into action.

One God—many ways of working

Open-minded readers of this book may have observed how God works through different agencies in the various parts of the world. In Latin America the Pentecostals have been the most significant instrument of the Holy Spirit, while in Korea and Indonesia the massive growth of the church has come largely through the Reformed churches. In West Africa the churches planted by inter-denominational missions play important roles in the overall life of the church of God, while in East Africa the mainline Anglicans and Lutherans host the revival work of the Holy Spirit. In Malaysia and Singapore the charismatic renewal has brought new life to the Methodists and Anglicans with considerable church growth as a result. In Europe too the charismatic movement has played a highly significant part in the whole development of church life and its churches often spearhead church growth in various of our countries.

Of course each of the above generalisations is too simplistic. In Latin America many other churches besides the Pentecostals show considerable growth. In West Africa the mainline denominations cannot be ignored, while in East Africa the Africa Inland Church was founded by an interdenominational mission and has become one of the largest churches of that area. In no part of the world can God be pigeon-holed to such a degree that he can only work in one particular type of church.

It is important to note that our God is bigger than just our favourite type of Christianity. Some Christian literature dismisses the charismatic renewal as a maverick and temporary phenomenon of no great significance. This is just not true to the facts. In many parts of the world it is the charismatic and Pentecostal churches which flourish more than others. But some other Christian literature is equally one-sided in its emphasis that God only works significantly through charismatic churches. The facts of our contemporary world deny this equally. Not only are most of the huge fast-growing Reformed churches of Korea and Indonesia not charismatic, but in Latin America too many anti-charismatic churches catch our attention with their vitality and growth.

When one travels to other countries, denominational flexibility and the ability to appreciate other expressions of the Christian faith become particularly important. Denominations which are centre-stage in one country may be quite peripheral in another; Christian movements which have a good name in one area may have a different history elsewhere and thus a different reputation.

Our responsibility

John Wesley affirmed that Christians should bend their backs to assist the work of the Holy Spirit. We have therefore to ask what the Holy Spirit is actually doing in the world today. Through the chapters of this book we have observed a little of God's activities in the various continents and among different peoples. Now our task is to work together with God in his mission. This will be achieved as we come to the Lord in prayer for the world and for his guidance as to what part he wants us to play.

As we have talked about different areas of the world we have noted not only the positive elements of what God has been doing, but also some of the negatives of what still remains to be done. We have felt the strengths of various churches around the world, but we have also grieved at some of the weaknesses. Such an awareness of the tremendous needs in our world can overwhelm us with a sense of our fearful inadequacy. What can little people like us do in the face of such pressures? But the knowledge of the world's and the church's needs can also stimulate us to a new sense of responsibility. God has not called us to become his disciples merely for our pleasure and salvation, but also in order to serve his church and the world. As we gain information about what God is doing in the world, our response whispers to God: 'Lord, what do you want me to do? I am ready to do anything anywhere for you.'

The New Testament states firmly, 'You are not your own; you were bought with a price' and then commands in consequence 'So glorify God in your body' (1 Cor 6:19, 20). In Jesus Christ God has paid an incalculable price for our salvation and has redeemed us for himself and for his service. The great purpose of our life now is to glorify God. It saddens us to observe how his name is dragged in the mud, blasphemed, misunderstood or ignored.

We long that people should honour him and love him as is his due. To this end we dedicate our lives.

Notes

1. P. Johnstone, *Operation World* (Send The Light: 1986).
2. M. Sinclair, *Ripening Harvest, Gathering Storm* (Monarch: 1988).
3. For further reading on the subject see the author's *What about other faiths?* (Hodder and Stoughton: 1989).
4. D. Barrett, *World Christian Encyclopaedia* (OUP: 1982).